Broken Into Position

Tameka L. Webb

ROYSTON
Publishing

BK Royston Publishing
P. O. Box 4321
Jeffersonville, IN 47131
502-802-5385
http://www.bkroystonpublishing.com
bkroystonpublishing@gmail.com

Cover Design: Gad Savage Elite Covers
Photographer: Tiera Owens of Aesthetic Ordonnance
Makeup Artist: Taryn Crawley of Flawless & Highly Favored Makeup Artistry
ISBN-13: 978-1-946111-82-1

Printed in the United States of America

CONTENTS

Letter to the Reader & My Intention

Hey Giirl!!!

As I sit here in what I call my Transformational Studio, I'm thinking about my intention for this — my first book.

Many of you don't know me. You don't know where I'm from, what I've been through. You don't know the amount of courage and strength it's taking right now to get these words out while facing the fear of judgment and exposure, not from the world, but from those closest to me. You don't know about my crazy/random personality that's helped me to push through tough times. You don't know about my many "whew...I can't believe I had the nerve to do that" moments — which have paid off tremendously.

I've had the nerve to finally figure out who I am, not who my family says I am or who my significant other says I am, but who God says I am.

I've had the nerve to say to myself, 'Although they're important, what about you? Don't you matter too? What about what you want? What about how you feel? You deserve to be happy too, right after you figure out what happiness is for you.'

I've overcome some things that could've taken some people out. Yes, I've cried, and yes, I've dealt with internal, physical and emotional side effects during the process, but I've come out on the other side and continue to strive to become a better version of myself.

I've had the nerve to make big, bold changes, do the seemingly impossible in the eyes of many, and achieve great personal success as a result, and I still truly believe that the best is yet to come.

Last but most definitely not ever least, I am reminded and continue to remind myself of the strong rock and unshakable foundation that I stand upon, the anchor that keeps me steady in the time of storms, my ever-present, all-knowing, lovingly merciful and gracious Savior, Jesus Christ.

So, here's my intention. I intend to bring you along with me as I candidly share my story for the first time of who I thought I was, what I went through and what I've become as a result of it all.

I pray that there's something in my story that resonates with you and helps you find the power that you've always had. I'll see you at the top — full of peace, self-actualization and fulfillment.

Tameka

Broken

Into

Position

Chapter 1

Ten Years Later and I'm Playing the Same Breakup CD

Chrisette Michele is singing "Blame it on me! Say it's my fault!"

"Well I think I'm just about over being your girlfriend!"

I'm shaking my head for real. I mean honestly, there I was AGAIN! Another relationship ending, listening to this same old CD. Chrisette, you're my girl, and I love your cd don't get me wrong. But it shouldn't still be applicable to me 10 years later.

Alright let's go back. I'll put down the spoon and half-empty jar of Nutella, take a breath and fill you in.

I'm single.

I'm divorced.

I'm 36 years old.

I don't have children.

This is not the life I'd planned.

I'm a Capricorn. I'm extremely organized. I'm an introvert and an empath. I love hard and I'm very ambitious. I'm strong on the outside. I have a poker face and I internalize my stress. I'd put the world on my back and carry it until it could stand on its own, if I could.

My father died about three years ago, and the man I thought was about to propose to me dumped me less than two weeks after my father passed. This was right after he'd met both sides of my family and all of my coworkers at our holiday party.

Wait, I need another spoonful of Nutella. Writing that just made me hangry (you know… hungry and angry at the same daggone time).

So, I was sitting here in my half-empty two-bedroom apartment with my dog, brainstorming this book and wondering how that had happened to me. That wasn't part of the plan. We were supposed to be together forever.

We were talking about enrolling in a first-time home buyer's class together. We had a checking account together to pay our bills. We made equal deposits, and I paid the bills…I forgot to mention that I used to be a control freak.

I cooked. I didn't clean, but I cooked.

I never said I was perfect.

I used to have a housekeeper, but I let her go when we decided to cohabitate. He was an OCD clean freak so we figured it'd work.

But anyway, I cooked! I gave him bubble baths from time to time. I did the grocery shopping. I prayed with and for him and encouraged him through ALL of the drama he had when we got together.

I was there for him through a messy divorce. DON'T JUDGE ME! He was already separated when he began pursuing me. Yes, I'm NOW clear on the fact that separated is still married, but I wasn't back then.

I was there for him through his child support process. This dude had like 15 court appearances. Talk about stress, but I was there for my man every step of the way. I mean, I'm divorced — I know the ropes.

I forgot to mention that I'd recently relocated for a new job. I moved two hours away from home for a wonderful opportunity, but don't forget that I'm kinda young. I was 33 at the time. I'm my mother's only child, and outside of college that was my first time away from Washington, DC. I was one of seven women in my organization and a minority.

So, I had stress of my own, underneath my poker face.

I was going to work every day feeling the pressure to prove myself, and then coming home to his stress every single day. And then he dumped me right after his divorce/child support were finalized and less than 2 weeks after my father died!

There were a bunch of curse words right here when I began writing this book. I mean, can you blame me?

He took me out to dinner and a movie just a couple weeks prior to our ending and asked me what kind of wedding I wanted, what kind of honeymoon ideas, and even started talking about a budget.

Oh, but it gets better. He told me I was beautiful like 25 times over dinner, saying we needed to hurry and start our family because we were both 33 years old. He wanted a daughter that looked just like me, with my eyes, hair and smile. This ninja was laying it on thick!

He voluntarily told my entire family on numerous occasions that he wanted to marry me, that he thanked God for me because I was the best thing that ever happened to him.

Remember, I'm my mother's only child. I have two younger siblings on my fathers' side. I'd just met my sister the year prior; she was 21 years old. We clicked immediately because we had so much in common. My brother was 8 years old. He's very smart and articulate, and he's a typical little boy who eats everything in sight and doesn't gain a pound. I have a wonderful maternal grandmother who's more like a second mother, my mother who's more like a crazy twin, four uncles, two aunts, and a host of cousins on my mother's side. My maternal grandfather passed away a few years before I was born. I have a feisty grandmother on my father's side, four uncles, three aunts, and a host of cousins. My fraternal grandfather passed away some years back.

He told ALL of these people, minus some cousins, about his intentions to love me forever.

Then wham! We're done. Did I miss something? #ScoopsNutella

My family and friends were all in shock and pissed for good reasons.

Everyone was asking questions, causing me to relive it over and over again.

I had to admit, my family and friends showed up when I needed them. My phone was ringing nonstop and I had a stream of text messages to respond to.

"What?! What happened?"

"Are you ok?"

"Come home this weekend!"

"Do I need to go fuck him up?!"

"That weak bitch!"

"He was ugly anyway. You can do better."

"Let's get drunk! I'll bring your favorite, Patron Silver!"

Then somehow my exes found out and started texting me.

"Do you want me to come over? You moved where? How often do you come home?"

"Damn baby! When was the last time you had some?"

"I thought you'd married him. You still think about me?"

All of that was too much so I decided to call my mother instead. She answered the phone on the first ring. "Hey baby! Are you ok?"

I never curse around my elders. That's how I was raised, but in that moment, I came out with it.

"I'm so fucking pissed! I was there for his ass through all of that bullshit, stressing me out nonstop and he does this?! I haven't been sexually satisfied in months, but I hung in there. Did I tell you his ass is cheap? Did you see my cheap-ass Christmas gift?! I know Christmas isn't about giving but you need to show me how much you love me, especially if you know that's one of my love languages. Just forget about what I want and how I feel, huh?!"

I realized that my mother hadn't said a word. She didn't interject with her usual, "It's going to be ok. I'm praying for you. Don't you have faith? It's going to work out in your favor."

That's probably because I was dropping the F-bomb, A-bomb, whatever other curse word bombs I'd dropped and because I was talking about sex.

I said "Hello?"

She busted out laughing and said, "DAMN! That's some bullshit!" We both laughed until it hurt and she let me finish venting. Once I finished, she said, "Well it seems like this worked out for the best because you weren't happy, but you were trying to be."

I agreed, but then that statement hit me like a ton of bricks. I'm strong; I'm self-aware, practically a know-it-all sometimes.

How did I not realize that I hadn't been happy all along?

Now that my wonderful mother had exposed me to myself, I was questioning everything.

Did I really love him?

Did I waste my time?

Did I purposefully ignore signs that would've prevented me from going through this mess?

Why did I allow someone with so much drama into my life? He came into my life with a shitload of baggage at a time when I was kinda thriving?

Was I desperate?

Did I have a self-esteem issue? I couldn't bring myself to put the "low" part in there, so we're gonna say self-esteem issue rather than low self-esteem. Help, Jesus!

You know what, I need wine and a full glass of it. This is too much for one night!

Is that damn Chrisette Michele CD still playing? I'd played the hell outta that CD when I was going through my divorce. I'd loved 't because every single song was talking about what I was dealing with, with my ex-husband.

But what the hell?! Hey Chrisette, why are you talking about my ex-boyfriend too?

Two different people, ten years apart, same CD...

Besides some of the same relationship problems, the only real thing these two men had in common was me.

Am I the problem?

I'm the common denominator.

Where's my glass?

Chapter 2

Bonnie & Clyde

I was a freshman in college and it was my first time away from home. My mother had me when she was very young, so my uncles were practically like fathers. Going away to college was all I could think about during my senior year in high school. There I was in New York, a few hours away from my home in Washington, DC, and you couldn't tell me anything.

I was barely legal and free from my strong-willed family who stressed straight A's and practically told me to become a computer programmer, so you know I was planning to do everything they told me not to do. First stop: guys and social media.

I created my account with an innocent screen name, and posted pics in my semi-fitted t-shirts, Alicia Keys cornrows, MAC lip gloss, tight GAP jeans, Eddie

Bauer coat...I'd always been a tomboy, but a girly tomboy if that makes sense.

One website in particular had a wall where people could post messages to you. It was there that I first met my Clyde. He posted a picture of a strawberry dripping chocolate onto a tongue. First thought: "Ooh he's nasty, no thanks!" It was probably two months later when he posted it again, but he said something this time that made me visit his page. What he said, I don't remember, but it must've been something good.

He was 5'10" with a chocolate complexion, muscular arms, a football player build and a bald head. He lived in DC and went to a school in Southeast where a few of my friends from junior high had attended. I asked them and no one knew him personally. All they recalled was that he was in ROTC and had been in a bad fight one day. He'd beaten the other boy up in the cafeteria which made me give him another look.

By the way, I'm from uptown DC. I'm 5'7" with a caramel complexion, medium light brown eyes that draw you in when I wear mascara or lashes, an inviting smile and a curvaceous figure.

I'd always had a thing for bad boys. It was sexy, I felt protected and it made me feel feminine. I could relax and just be because my man was taking care of things.

His look and the badass militant persona that my friends described made me want to respond, so I did. Plus, I figured we'd make some pretty coffee-complexioned babies.

We chatted every day until the 9/11 tragedy happened. The college I attended was less than an hour from Ground Zero. I had an uncle in New York City, another uncle that worked on Capitol Hill, and I didn't have reception on my Tracfone. It was 2001; yeah, I had a Tracfone. I was homesick and ended up getting strep throat twice, so I decided to move back to DC and transfer to a college near home.

I saw my Clyde every day for a couple years. He gave me the courage to stand up to my family, which still treated me like I was ten years old. Most of them hated him. They always told me to never date a man from Southeast, and never said why, so you know that made me want him more. My friends hated him too, because I didn't have time for them anymore — in my mind.

No one knew that my Clyde had proposed twice. I told him he was crazy because he didn't have a ring. Well, the second time he proposed he gave me one of his mothers' rings with these little cute diamond sprinkles that I wished I could see with the naked eye. He waited 3 months, bought a ring and proposed to me again on the subway one night after a date, saying that he was crazy about me. I said yes and started wearing the ring.

Petrified of what my family would say is an understatement. But forget about them for a minute, I didn't know if I was ready. I was 23 years old and hadn't experienced life, but I knew that I was in love. I felt invincible when I was with him. We were Bonnie and Clyde, the two of us against the world and no one could tell me otherwise.

We got married, a small shotgun wedding on Valentine's Day. My grandmother and mother approved because they wanted me to stop "fornicating and shacking up."

I grew up in church. My grandmother was a deaconess and my mother sang in the choir, so the idea of eliminating some sin from my life felt pretty good.

Everything seemed perfect. We had so much fun together. We were best friends, tag team partners; we fed off of one another's energy. We were very playful! One of my favorite pranks was to pour a glass of ice-cold water over the top of the shower curtain while he showered, right onto his bald head. I'd turn the bathroom light off and run out laughing, while he gasped for air and begged me to turn the light back on. He'd step out of the shower to turn the light on and find me hiding beside the door with another glass of ice water. Splash, right in the face! I'd try to run away. He'd catch me. We'd end up in bed, sheets soaked and half of the apartment wet.

But…no one knew that we also had really bad arguments, and he had a hard time controlling his anger.

When we disagreed, things would escalate. He'd get close to my face screaming and cursing at me, demanding respect.

The first couple times it totally caught me off guard. Who is this person? It shocked me, hurt my feelings and made me want to lash out, which was a feeling that I wasn't used to. Sure, the men in my family told me what to do and were pretty strict, but they were kind. Their criticism came from a loving place.

Clyde was verbally abusive.

I'll never forget one evening in particular. At the time I was working at a bank full-time and going to school in the evenings, and Clyde was working a third shift. I had just dropped him off at work, and then I got right on the phone with him and talked with him for my entire drive home.

When I got home, I tried to relax and began talking to my best girlfriend on the phone. She was technically the only friend I had left. He called me on the house phone, so I told my best friend to hold on and answered the other line. He told me to get off the phone with her and talk to him. He'd truly isolated me and tried his best to end my last remaining friendship. I told him that I'd call him back before I went to bed, which would be soon, because I wanted to talk to my friend. We were just together like 20 minutes ago, and we'd just got off the phone because we talked while I drove home. So, I did what I'd recently started doing, which was hang up on him.   I wanted a few minutes for myself; it seemed like the only time that wasn't consumed with him was when I was asleep or at work.

Whenever I'd mustered up the courage to hang up on him, he'd usually call me back to back until I answered the phone. This time was different.

He didn't call me at all, but 20 minutes later, while I was lying across the bed laughing with my friend, I heard a loud boom. My friend even heard it. I got quiet trying to figure out what the heck the noise was. I didn't have to wait too long because I heard it again. BOOM! Then I saw what it was.

Clyde had driven home in the work vehicle, busted through the front door, kicked in the bedroom door and ripped the phone cord out of the wall. He came over to me while I was laying there in shock, yelling and cursing at me in my face about him being my husband and that I had to respect him. He demanded that every time he called, I'd better drop whoever and whatever and talk to him.

I stood up after a minute of that because I felt too submissive and at a disadvantage lying in the bed, with a grown man over me yelling like that.

He grabbed me by the shoulders and roughly threw me down on the bed and kept yelling and cursing at me.

This time was different. I blacked out. I could see his lips moving but I couldn't hear him. I could tell that he was still saying the same stuff and wasn't gonna stop. What he didn't know is that he'd activated the fighter inside of me. It was like he'd pressed the "On" button on my "Fight Mode," and he'd pressed it so hard I was stuck on.

I stood up again and walked up to this face, nose to nose and I told him that the day he touched me like that again would be the day that he'd die. Not that I was gonna call my hot-tempered mother, my father or any of my uncles — that I'd take him out myself. He stood there for a few seconds, turned around and went back to work.

I'd found my voice, and I was so proud of myself, but I was still shaken up.

This wasn't love.

I went for a drive so I could get myself together. I couldn't tell my mother or anyone in my family, so I called my best friend. As soon as I started telling her she said hold on and dialed another one of our friends on a three-way call. They started saying what they were gonna do, that they were coming to get me and my stuff. I hung up and kept driving and started crying.

They didn't understand; they didn't get it. I was married. They'd never been married. I didn't have anywhere to go. My family would find out, and none of them liked him. He knew where I worked. The apartment and bills were in both of our names. The list goes on and on. I felt alone and I felt stuck.

All I could do was pray:

Jesus, what just happened?

This man is supposed to love me.

I'm so confused! I know that this hurts but I don't feel it.

I know that I'm suppressing it because I have to be strong right now.

Lord, make me strong.

Make me resilient.

Bless my marriage.

Bless my husband.

In Jesus' name I pray, Amen.

This went on for years.

I became a professional arguer. He'd pick a fight, and I'd piss him off so bad that he'd start throwing things at the wall, punching holes in the walls and doors. If our arguments were rated on a scale of 1 – 10, he'd start with a 5 and I was at level 10. He'd increase to a 7 and I was still at 10. We'd call each other names and verbally abuse one another. I used to try to cut him with my words because he was hurting me so bad, I wanted him to feel how I was trying not to feel.

I didn't tell anyone.

In spite of it all, we had sex six days a week. I still wasn't satisfied. It was my responsibility to keep our sex life spicy. Between the arguments, his list of insecurities and "my inability to get pregnant," the tension became so thick that it felt like we were posing in our marriage. I know I was. I know he wanted a child, and I know he blamed me, thinking there was something wrong with me.

I went to three different doctors, where I received three clean bills of health and three recommendations for my husband to get evaluated. He refused and continued to blame me. Two of the doctors respectfully told me that he might not be the one for me. I guess they discerned that there was trouble behind our paradise facade.

All of this drove me closer to God. I started praying more, and I attended church on and off. Clyde would only go once or twice a year. Lord forbid if the pastor preached about anything that was applicable to our situation. He'd swear I'd told someone at whatever church we were visiting (keyword: *visiting*), ruining the remainder of my Sunday. In short, I didn't mind attending church alone.

One day his behavior changed. I'm an observer. I watch for a while to validate what I'm seeing and feeling.

Red Flag! I got on my knees beside the bed while he was sleeping.

Jesus, something isn't right.

I know that something isn't right.

I've been a good wife. I haven't cheated, even though this man has hurt me and I don't feel fulfilled in this marriage.

If something is going on, show me.

Show me, regardless of how much it might hurt.

Show me and let me make up my mind on how to move forward.

In Jesus' name I pray, Amen.

That night, He showed me.

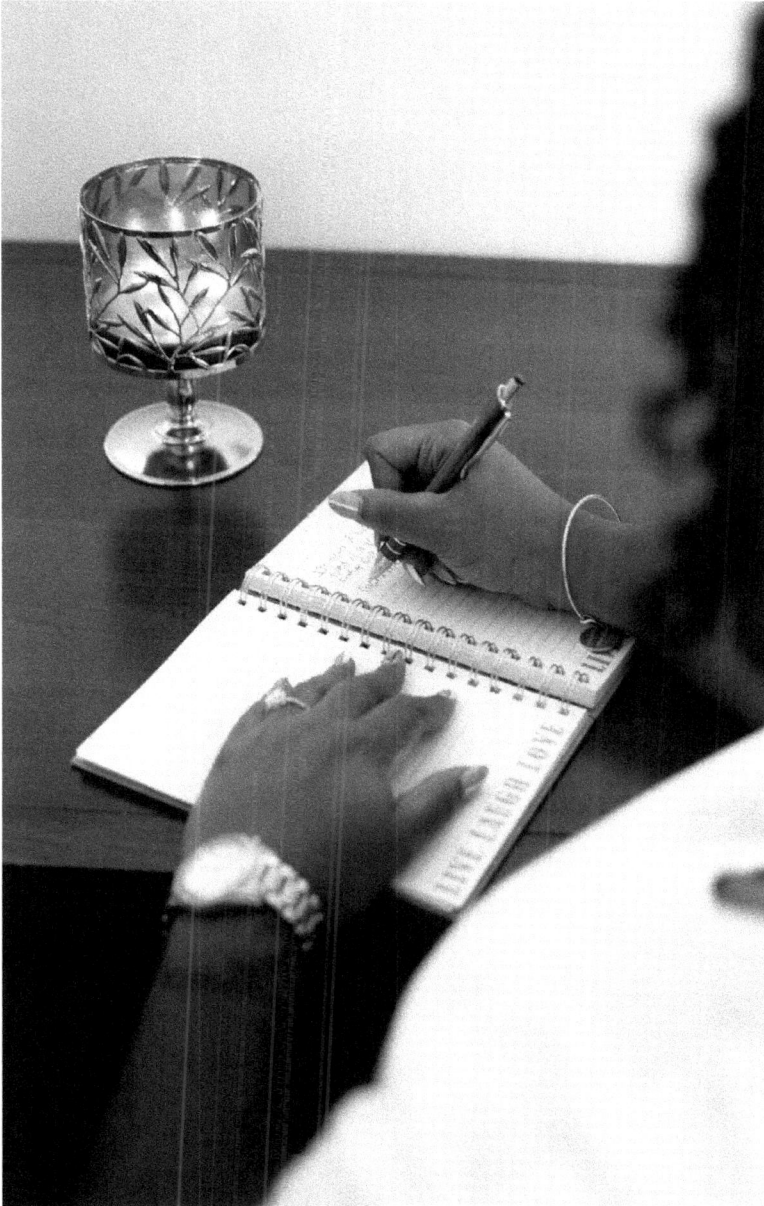

Chapter 3

So…What Now?

It was 3 a.m. on the night that I prayed for God to show me. I wasn't dreaming. I literally woke up and heard, "Check his phone." My husband was asleep beside me.

Lord, is this you?

I'm going back to sleep.

"Check his phone."

Lord, I know I prayed for this.

I don't check phones…ever!

If this is You, I'll check it once.

I got up, grabbed his phone and went into the bathroom.

There it was — what I'd felt, what I sensed, what I'd prayed for.

Over 40 text messages coming in, over 40 text messages going out, pictures and videos of my husband and three different women. Nude pics and videos of him masturbating, messages arranging lunches at their jobs, him giving the women directions to our home. He even told one chick that his wife is friends with the next-door neighbor, so she should walk around back and come through the patio door.

So, that's why the patio door was unlocked last week.

I walked out of the bathroom. I remembered that it was cold outside, so I put sweatpants on top of my pajama bottoms. I put a hoodie on top of my pajama top, pulled my boots on, grabbed my purse and dropped both of our cellphones inside. I grabbed the laptop, my car keys and his (we had two cars at the time), and walked out the front door.

I warmed my car up for a few minutes and drove to a gas station maybe 10 minutes away and pulled out my wallet. I called every bank and credit card company, telling them that my husband and I were in

Atlantic City, that he'd lost his wallet and that they should cancel all his cards. My next stop was the ATM. I withdrew the max amount from each account. I believe this was a Saturday night/Sunday morning, so all he'd have was whatever cash he had on him, until Monday.

I drove to the highway, I-495N, heading to my mother's house. I was probably driving 95 mph; my adrenaline was pumping, and I was internalizing everything. I called my mother to let her know I was coming and what I'd discovered. Thank God my mother is a night owl. She said, "WHAT?! I'm unlocking the door. I know you, please stop speeding. We'll talk about it when you get here. Please focus on the road."

I called his mother. She was asleep, so I had to call four times.

After apologizing for waking her, I told her what I'd discovered. She apologized over and over and said she'd get his ass. She asked me where I was going. I told her that I didn't want to talk about it and that I'd call her later.

When I hung up from her, it sunk in. My husband had been cheating on me!

I pulled over in a parking lot and called my best guy friend in Chicago that I hadn't spoken to in years. It must've been 3 a.m. his time. He answered, and I broke down crying and screaming in heartbreaking pain that I just knew would kill me.

How could he have done this to me, after all these years and everything we'd been through? I'd done things for him that I'd never imagined myself doing for anyone.

My best guy friend, we'll call him Eugene, had a girlfriend. They lived together. After I said all that I could say, I apologized for being disrespectful by calling at that hour. Both Eugene and his girlfriend empathized, and they told me to leave everything, come to Chicago right now and get a fresh start. They even said they'd help me find a job there.

Choices.

We hung up after I told them I'd keep that offer in my back pocket for now.

My poker face returned as I walked into my mother's house. I had to tell the story again, and of course she was pissed. Since I was hurt and angry, I thought about telling her about the verbal abuse but decided not to. Then my cellphone rang. It was Clyde's ass.

I said, "Hello," as mean and cold as I could.

It was probably 5 a.m., so he was supposed to be getting ready for work at his new job. Surprise! No wife, no cellphone, no car keys.

He said in a perky voice, "Hey baby! Where are you?"

I screamed, "What the fuck do you mean, where am I?! What phone are you calling me on?! Where's your cellphone?!" I'd never yelled at someone like that before. It was as if my pain was unleashed and coming from the pit of my stomach, with all the volume and bass I could muster. My mother looked like she'd seen a ghost, got up and left the room to give me privacy.

He tried to play it off, like he didn't know what was going on until I blew my stack again. I told him about all that I'd seen in the phone while he acted surprised and lied.

I hung up on him.

He called back with a fake sad voice, asking why I'd hung up.

I hung up again.

He called back again, this time he was pissed and started yelling at me. I put it on speaker this time, hoping my mother would hear. I told him that I would keep hanging up until he grew some balls and told the truth.

He was quiet for long time on the phone. Then he admitted most of it, but denied that he ever had anyone in our car or in our apartment.

I said, "So you know we're done, right?"

It was his turn to cry, and he did, hysterically. I hung up and powered both phones off while I cried to my mother.

I stayed there for three days. My mother parked my car in the garage and told him I wasn't there every time he called. She told him that she knew I was upset but didn't know why, then asked him what happened. He said they could talk about it later.

I finally prayed about it, cried and then cried some more and eventually convinced myself that the pain in my chest and stomach weren't detrimental.

I was experiencing my first heartbreak.

We met at IHOP for breakfast on day four.

He looked like shit. I enjoyed that.

He cried as soon as he saw me. He talked through the tears, while I looked at him without speaking with a blank stare.

He'd never seen me be so cold. I had always been very happy, optimistic and relaxed, or verbally combative when we argued. I was never this cold and nonchalant. I just kept staring at him. My leg started doing a nervous bounce, and he got silent. My fidgeting increased, and the tears started to fall. He stopped crying, and I saw him realize the magnitude of what he'd done. We talked about it and decided that we needed counseling.

I moved back in and kicked myself every day for weeks. I smoked a cigarette — I wasn't a smoker. I drank hard liquor and watched him try to sleep in fear the first few nights. That amused me and angered me at the same time. Two months after I returned, he decided that counseling was stupid. The counselor always took my side, and it wasn't "fair."

I played Chrisette Michele's *Epiphany* CD on repeat while I commuted for an hour to work and another hour home every day.

I was physically present at home, but I didn't want to be there. The hurt that I experienced had numbed me. I didn't want to be there. I didn't want him anymore. The person that I trusted without borders had hurt me more than I could've ever fathomed. I didn't want to be divorced. I didn't want that red D on my chest…that scarlet letter…but I wanted out!

In November of 2009 I told Clyde that I was leaving on my birthday, December 31st. He needed to figure out his living arrangements, get a roommate, something…I didn't care because I was leaving.

On January 21, 2010, I moved in with my grandmother. I took only my clothes, one big screen television, and one of our two dogs, which broke my heart.

So…what now?

Chapter 4

I'm a Player!

There I was, sleeping in my childhood bedroom at my grandmother's house. My entire life was crammed into one room that seemed so much smaller than I remembered.

All I could think about was my old home with my husband: the space that I hadn't appreciated, the privacy, oh, and the man holding me every night, kissing me every morning and night — the good times that we had.

Although I didn't want him sexually toward the end, I sure wanted him or someone now. It was like a drought in the desert. Somebody come water these crops before I go crazy!

I had gained so much weight during our courtship and marriage. Don't act like you don't know — you start a new relationship, and you both gain that "happy weight." I was looking very happy, but I wasn't feeling it. I was crying myself to sleep most nights and unhappy in every category I could think of.

Fortunately, my grandmother's house was ten minutes from my job. That was wonderful. The only problem was I didn't have a car. I soon realized that public transportation and weight gain don't mix, especially in the snow. I was miserable!

I had to fix something immediately!

I joined a gym and went faithfully Monday-Friday, right after work. I cooked and packed my meals every day, which helped me to lose 35 pounds in two months.

Although it'd been a while, I called all my friends that I'd neglected for years. Most of them had some words for me, but all accepted my apologies. I regained my social life.

Clyde came to my grandmother's house once a week for the first 2-3 months, begging me to come home. I prayed and journaled daily to resist his prompts and it helped. I was feeling better about myself with my weight loss, but my hormones were raging! After all, I was a married woman; I hadn't gone this long without, umm, "physical activities" since I started dating my husband. My attitude was out of this world at times, and I couldn't take my mind off of getting physical.

You know what comes next...well, maybe you do.

It was a rainy night and Clyde had come to my grandmother's house. He said he just wanted to see me and spend some time together. I agreed.

He sat on the sofa. I sat on the loveseat. My grandmother was upstairs and asleep. We talked about life. He asked for a hug. I agreed and it felt so good. He smelled so familiar. I felt so relaxed in his arms. He held me tight and I squeezed him back. He kissed me like he hadn't seen me in years. I was hungry for him in every way and I couldn't hide it. He was all over me and I didn't try to stop him. He went home feeling optimistic that night. I went to bed confused.

I had sex with my husband, and that's how it felt, like sex and not like lovemaking. I hadn't forgotten our history — I deserved better, I wanted better and I still wasn't sexually satisfied.

That night I prayed. I told God how sad and confused I was. I felt empty, like I didn't know who I was. I knew that I was Clyde's wife, but it felt like I'd given up whatever identity I once had when I married him. I'd just become "his," and now that I was leaving him, I was leaving all that now defined me. I asked God to show me who I was, show me my purpose, show me who He created me to be.

I woke up that morning and heard God say, "Hey Giirl!" My first thought was, 'Hey God! I love you. I know you hear me!' He said, "No, Hey Giirl is your business."

God had given me a clear vision and some insight on my purpose. Let's be honest — that petrified me!

I put it in my notes on my phone and carried on with my day. I didn't feel qualified, nor did I think it was the right time. I had too much going on and did not have time or resources to start a business, or so I thought.

I went to the grocery store after the gym later that week, and I met a guy. He followed me around the store for a bit, flirting, which made my armpits sweat. He was tall, had milk chocolate skin, a bald head, perfect white teeth, wore glasses and was dressed professionally. He had a football player build, maybe a quarterback. This man made me want to drool. We exchanged numbers, and he offered to walk me home with my groceries, saying that he lived across the street. I'd just purchased an older car because I was tired of riding the bus, so I politely declined saying that I was driving. He walked me to my car and put my groceries in the trunk — brownie point.

We texted and talked in the evenings for over a month. I liked it but I was still very hurt and upset about my circumstances, making excuses about why I couldn't go out him. I prayed that I wouldn't see him but couldn't resist answering his calls and texts. I came clean one day, telling h m what I had going on. He took it well, surprisingly, and invited me over for dinner.

I have a weakness for tall men. I'm 5'7," add a pair of heels and I'm almost six feet tall. When that 6'4" man opened the door, I had to try to remember how to give a sexy smile and flirt. It'd been so long. I'm guessing I was successful; he grabbed me by the waist and pulled me close for a hug. I know I moaned out loud.

He had one candle lit on the dining room table and some type of covers over the lamps to dim the lighting in the rest of the living room area of his apartment. So,

I'd say the ambiance was nice. The dinner he'd cooked was delicious, and the conversation was great.

I was shaking like a leaf.

Two glasses of wine later, he suggested that we watch a movie in the bedroom. I followed him and stopped in front of the bed, letting him know that I was nervous, that I'd been with the same man for eight years, that I don't do these kinds of things, rambling on and on. He approached me again, and I felt my upper lip start to sweat. He picked me up, kissed me and threw me on the bed.

Even after my weight loss, I'm still a thick girl. Suffice it to say I hadn't felt this turned on in years. He undressed me slowly and kissed every inch of my entire body. When I was uncomfortably butt naked, he asked me to undress him. I could handle that. He held me for a while, we talked, and then he asked if I was ready. I said yes. He was gentle and patient, yet masculine, then aggressive. He took me to a place I hadn't been before, then again in the shower as we washed each other off. He asked me to stay, but I needed to go check on my grandmother and walk my dog, so I left.

As I drove home, I compared how I was feeling with him…we'll call him Grocery Store Boy…to how I felt with my husband. That probably wasn't the best of ideas, but I felt fulfilled and happy in the sex category for the first time in years!

Grocery Store Boy and I continued to see each other for a couple months, until one day we got into the shower together and there was a ball of women's hair in the corner, like a woman had washed her hair and cleaned it out of the drain. I was still numb emotionally so I got dressed and left. I had no feelings and nothing to lose. Goodbye, Grocery Store Boy.

Clyde was still calling, stopping by my job and my grandmother's house. He knew that something was different with me.

Guys started approaching me frequently. I'd go on dates and hang out with my girlfriends. I decided to enjoy life, while keeping my clothes on for a bit.

A couple months went by, and it was time to get my car inspected. The manager approached me while I was standing in the wrong line to pick up my car. He showed me to my car and flirted like his life depended on it. We can call him Tow Truck Boy. He said that he saw his future in my eyes, and then pulled a thick wad of cash out of his pocket to show me. I replied dryly, saying "Interesting." Money doesn't impress me unless it directly benefits me.

Tow Truck Boy had two full-time jobs (at the city car inspection facility and driving a tow truck at night), and he owned a large house and four or five cars. We dated and spent most evenings and nights together. He liked to smoke weed and drink on occasion. I was more of a social drinker but ended up smoking with him a couple nights a week. We'd smoke, go to a lounge where he knew the owner, sit in the VIP section and people watch. He ended up having "baby mama drama," so I cut him off.

I'd gone from sad and confused to amused and assertive.

Chapter 5

Angel Dust

I seemed to meet a new guy everywhere I went. I met two guys, on separate occasions of course, when I was leaving parties. Both were tall with light brown skin and attractive. We'll call them Chrysler Boy and Incognito Boy.

Chrysler Boy had light brown eyes and silky curly hair. He was muscular, a little thick and had luscious soft lips. He owned his home, had a souped-up Chrysler 300 with monitors in the headrests and on the dashboard, and dark tinted windows. He also owned a motorcycle. He played the guitar, had a deep voice and was a bad boy of course. It was not surprising to go out with him, get back to his place and see a gun or merchandise that he was selling on the coffee table in the middle of the living room. He'd apologize, put everything away and resume hanging on my every word and move until he fell asleep. He'd insist that we had to be touching one another every second that we were together. He'd try to hold me hostage at his house for days. I wasn't complaining, but I had to actively remind myself to not feel anything for him besides physical attraction. Due to his profession, he eventually had to "go away for a little while."

Incognito Boy had a solid and slim basketball player build. He looked like a combination of two rappers: Common and T.I. He always looked fresh out of a magazine, dressed in the latest sneakers, jeans, t-shirt and coordinating fitted caps. He always had a short and fresh haircut and walked like he couldn't put his legs together. We hung out for months. I attended a couple of his family functions, spent time with his friends and he met mine. I even met his two daughters who were always dressed like models; he was a full-time single dad. I was at his job one night. He worked overnight, and we were standing outside at his truck talking. I had my back to him, and I was leaning back on his chest. He had his arms wrapped around me and whispered into my ear that it'd been months, and he wanted to know if we were ever going to have sex. I laughed until it hurt. I had tears streaming down my face, leaning over holding my legs laughing. I laughed so hard and for so long, he started laughing too. I was petrified! I was starting to like him, but again I felt guilty, so I smiled and said yes one day soon. I hadn't been completely honest with him. He didn't know I was married, and it turns out that he hadn't been completely honest with me either.

I tried to limit the amount of time that I spent with him from then on. We hadn't talked about sex before, not once in months. We just hung out and had drinks, or he'd call me and say come chill with me. If I had one of my girlfriends with me, I'd tell him to bring a friend, and we'd play cards and just have fun.

Then one day, you see, what happened was…well, let's just say that alcohol will make you let your guard down. He didn't push me into it. It just happened naturally, and I think it blew both of our minds. I now understood why he walked like that. He was so humble. I think I avoided him for over a month after that night. I told one of my girlfriends that I should probably stay away from him because I didn't want to get addicted and catch feelings.

I was on my lunch break one day when he called and I decided to answer. He said, "Dag Tameka, for real?" I said, "What?" He expressed that he felt like he'd disappointed me that night and wanted to know how I felt. I laughed a little and reassured him that I was far from disappointed. I just had a lot going on, not to mention the fact that I realized I was missing Chrysler Boy.

Incognito Boy and I started seeing one another again. I knew that I had to tell him because he had a right to know, so one night as we were about to go into his cousin's house, I told him that I was married but separated. He looked shocked, walked away and left me standing outside. I had one of my girlfriends with me, who was already inside having fun with his family.

I felt stuck. I knew he was pissed and probably needed some space, but my friend was there. Plus, I didn't want to leave him or end our night on a sour note, so I leaned against my car and called him. He answered the phone and said, "What?!" I asked him to come outside; I wanted to talk. He walked up to me looking surprised and let down. I explained what I'd been through with my husband, why I left and that I was afraid to tell him. He grabbed me, held me tight, apologizing for what had happened to me, and took me inside.

It felt like no one else was in the room for most of the night. He stared at me, played in my hair and kissed me. His eldest daughter came over and sat in his lap, smiling at me. He held her and tried to contain his smile while she and I interacted. Then she said, "Tameka, we love you!" and ran away. That caught the both of us off guard.

My girlfriend, Incognito Boy's brother and one of his cousins said they were going outside. It was dark so I gave my friend the look like, "Where are you going, ma'am, and what are you about to do?" Incognito Boy motioned for me to come and go outside with him and them too. All of the guys started smoking weed, except for Incognito Boy, which I liked. I asked him just to confirm that he doesn't smoke. I mean I'd never seen him smoke before, so I was just looking for him to confirm what I felt like I knew. He said, "I don't smoke what I sell." What?! We'd been spending time together for months. I'd been to his full-time job. I mean, he was always dressed well and his children too. He did have a couple of vehicles, but wait a minute…he'd been holding back too. We went back inside to talk, and he opened up about all of his streams of income. I started to feel like that was my type. That's what I'd been unknowingly attracting. I wasn't sure if I liked that, but I did like "feeling safe" and knowing that my guy was good financially.

I'd been drinking slowly but consistently throughout the night. My girlfriend didn't drive, and it was really late. One of his cousins gave Incognito Boy and I his bedroom, and my friend reluctantly slept sitting up on the sofa beside his generous cousin that she was obviously not interested in. She liked his brother who had left a few hours earlier. She managed to whisper to me, "YOU OWE ME BIG FOR THIS!!!" She was half smiling; I laughed a little and promised to make it up to her.

We stayed for a few more hours, until the sun came up. Although my girlfriend had made her sofa stay look a little funny, I knew she was uncomfortable, so I started my exit. She immediately took my car keys and went to wait for me in the car. Incognito Boy laughed and said she was a good friend. His cousin had been trying to make a move all night, while she playfully fought him off like an older woman who was secretly interested. Incognito Boy walked me to my car. With sober minds, we both looked at one another; we had new information to process. We hugged and left one another as usual, but I knew things would be different.

Chapter 6

Stalkers

One of my girlfriends had been determined to get me out of my "separation funk." I knew that I needed to file for a divorce soon. I was clear that I wanted one but became extremely sad every time the thought crossed my mind. This girlfriend figured that the solution was to go clubbing. I was willing to try almost anything. I mean, I had been on a strict "work and focus on my husband diet" for years. I was perfectly okay with going to a club. We ended up clubbing six nights every week. I could barely function at work. I was so sleepy, and my knees hurt from dancing so much. I kept post-club snacks in my car just in case, and we even had designated sections at certain places. We got to know the owners and bartenders, and they always hooked us up. There was one club/lounge type of spot that we went to once a week. Two of the security guards were always in my face.

Both were about six feet tall, dark chocolate colored skin and straight white teeth. One was all muscle, maybe 200 pounds. The other one had more weight, maybe 250. They always had two or three guys with them. One was 100% my type: about 6'4," caramel complexion, football player build, curly hair — y'all should know by now. The three of them would flirt with me. The smaller security guard was very laid back and quiet, but the bigger guard would inappropriately smack my butt, aggressively grab me and put his hands in my hair saying he could tell I liked it rough. This happened every Friday, every week. Sometimes about eight of us would leave the lounge when it closed and go to a bar a few blocks away. It was on the top floor of an office building. We'd stay there from midnight or 1 a.m. until whenever, laughing, dancing and just enjoying life. The bigger security guard became too much for me to tolerate. He was too rough and flirted with every woman that looked halfway decent. The caramel complexioned friend had a girlfriend, and the quiet guard was too shy, so in my mind, all of them were cool but irrelevant.

Then you see what had happened was...just joking. Then I found out that I needed to have surgery. It was a minor procedure, but I needed to be put to sleep for the first time in my life, and I was petrified! I told my girlfriend, AKA my clubbing partner. She told me everything would be okay, but we needed to really "turn up" the night before my procedure.

I got so drunk! She kept buying me drinks and accepting free drinks for us, and I kept drinking.

I had overdone it. I tapped her when the lounge was closing and told her I couldn't stand up, let alone walk up the 15 steps to get outta there. Oh, and who was gonna drive? We came in my car, and she lived in Baltimore, about an hour away. The two security guards and their friends came over to check on me and help me. I don't remember much except for them telling me I was going to be okay and the shy one taking me to my car. He walked me to my car much slower than needed, told me that my girlfriend was gonna drive me home and asked for my phone number. All I could do was look at him and wish he were either Chrysler Boy or Incognito Boy. He called his phone from my phone, and gave my phone back to me. He must've taken the phone out of my hand because I don't remember giving it to him. I had my procedure. My husband and my mother went with me. He insisted on coming and seemed genuinely concerned, but I'd lost all respect and trust for him, and I knew it would never come back.

A couple days later, I received a text from the shy security guard. He was checking on me. Let's call him Pizza Boy...I'll explain later.

Pizza Boy and I texted for a few weeks, then eventually started talking on the phone while I was at home recovering. He seemed like a nice person. I could tell he had a hot temper if provoked, but I never thought that we would be anything or that I would ever have to deal with that from him. His only job was doing security a few nights a week at the lounge. He lived with his mother and he didn't drive. He was very humble and low key, which was refreshing and not what I was used to.

Eventually I went back to the club with my girlfriend. It felt good to have fun and see my Friday night friends. Pizza Boy would come into the main area and look at me from time to time, and go back to his post.

That night when I got home, he texted me saying he wanted to spend some time with me soon. I agreed and we ended up sitting in my car, laughing and talking, just enjoying one another's company. He told me he was antisocial and an introvert, mainly talking to the people he knows and devoting his time and energy to his woman and his daughter. He had a little girl that lived with his ex-girlfriend.

Chrysler Boy was still, umm, "away" due to his work, and Incognito Boy and I spoke from time to time. Things were different between us and I decided to be okay with that.

Pizza Boy and I ended up spending a lot of time together for months, which I wasn't expecting and I'm sure none of the guys at our Friday night spot would expect it either. He was so low key, wore his uniform and was just quiet. He flew under the radar and was softening my heart.

Since I saw him as a potential friend initially, I opened up about my marriage and the guys I'd been talking to. He told me about his ex and why they didn't work out.

One day he looked different to me. It was like I saw him for the first time, not as the security guard friend but as Pizza Boy.

He was taller than me, smooth and soft dark chocolate skin, medium build and all muscle, broad shoulders, straight perfect white teeth, and Chinese looking eyes that completely disappeared when he smiled or laughed. He had nice sizeable lips and huge hands. I was like, "Well damn, I didn't see all of this before!"

He had some ideas for businesses but didn't seem to have the drive to get anything done.

I had started traveling with my girlfriends and trying to live my best life regardless of any situation with men. I told him what I liked to do for fun, that I liked to shop, buy expensive purses, keep my hair and nails done, and go to upscale restaurants and events. He said okay. I was trying to let him know, without saying it, that I thought he was cool but I wasn't sure how we'd fit into each other's worlds.

We continued to spend time together. I kept going to the same lounge, and no one knew that he and I were friends. Even though I'd talk to him on my way in and on my way out of the lounge, he couldn't come inside, so no one saw us interact.

One non-clubbing night, he and I were watching a movie at his house and he awkwardly kissed me. It was so awkward I felt sorry for him. He was nervous as hell and obviously unsure if I felt the same way. I leaned in, cupped one of his cheeks with one of my hands and kissed him once on the lips. He wasn't a good kisser but he tried. I thought it was cute and it helped me to let my guard down. He was extra careful about touching me. He held my attention. He was patient, understanding and attentive. His big hands caressed every inch of my body, and his soft and sizable lips did an excellent job of kissing every piece of me, except for the lips on my face. Then he slowed down even more and really took his time with me. We enjoyed one another all night, and I slept on his chest wearing a smile I had not expected.

When we woke up the next morning, he was upbeat and extra happy. I laughed and avoided the "So what now?" thought that kept trying to creep into my mind.

The night before had been different. It wasn't just the physical act. I felt something that I'd been trying to avoid for a year or so. I was developing feelings for him.

As he walked me to my car, he carried the conversation by himself. I was peaceful and felt safe, deciding to think about it when I was alone at home.

After he closed my car door, he said, "You know you fucked up, right?" That caught me completely off guard.

I tried to smile, assuming he was joking and said, "What?" He said, "You fucked up by giving me that goodness. Now you ain't never getting rid of me."

A few weeks later, Pizza Boy got a job — as an assistant manager at a pizza chain restaurant.

By then we had made it "official." He was the boyfriend of a separated woman.

My husband had decreased his visits to my grandmother's house and to my job, which made Pizza Boy happy. It made me happy too because I'd started praying for my husband to move on. My heart would never allow me to consider trying our relationship again, but I still wanted him to be happy.

I'm pretty sure my husband must've been parked at my grandmother's house and possibly caught a glimpse of Pizza Boy and me, because suddenly he completely switched up on me.

He started calling and texting, cursing me out, saying go be with whomever you're dealing with. He changed his profession and invited me to an awards ceremony. He was receiving an award and wanted me to be on his arm. I told him that wouldn't be a good idea, that I was about to finally file for a divorce.

He didn't handle my response well.

I constantly worried about my husband and Pizza Boy seeing one another face-to-face. I would frequently ask Pizza Boy how he would handle it, that if it were to happen, I'd want him to just ignore my husband and keep moving. He tried to reassure me that I had nothing to worry about because he'd be cool until my husband either touched me or him, or insulted me. Then, he'd kill him.

Every time I thought about that, which was frequently, I'd get a visual of them fighting to the death

— a fight that I could do nothing about, besides call 9-1-1. A fight that I'd caused because I didn't wait until I was divorced before starting another relationship. The thought and visualization scared me and made me feel sick.

Pizza Boy knew that I was stressing about filing for a divorce and decided to surprise me. He told me to pack a bag for the weekend and stand outside of my grandmother's house. Although surprises are cute, I was too much of a control freak to relax.

I stood on the sidewalk in form-fitting denim capris. They were fitted in the waist, butt and hips, then dropped straight down from there. I was wearing an off-the-shoulder olive green top, with gold hoop earrings and gold sandals. I had a huge MCM tote bag on my shoulder, a gold watch, one gold bracelet and a gold locket. My lip gloss was shining, and I tried to enjoy the spring breeze on my skin while I waited. I leaned down to pull up the handle on my patent leather, forest green, rolling tote bag and heard a car horn honking.

Pizza Boy pulled up in a car he'd rented for the weekend, singing "Beauty" by Dru Hill to me while it played through the car stereo. Did I mention that Pizza Boy could sing?

I smiled so hard and felt so special. A couple of my grandmother's neighbors were outside and saw him. He got out of the car half way through the song, escorted me to the front passenger's seat and put my bag in the trunk. He took me to the beach. He'd made a reservation at a five-star hotel, which surprised me again. He truly treated me like a queen the entire weekend.

The following Friday we decided to go to the lounge, so we could actually go inside and hang out together. I forgot to mention that he'd quit working there when he started working at the restaurant.

He dressed up and got there before me. I was still at work when he called, saying everyone was surprised to see him and even more surprised to see him dressed up and being social.

I arrived about an hour or so later. As I walked down the steps into the lounge, greeting our friends, he spotted me from across the room, came over and hugged me. All of the usual guys and our friends seemed to say "WOW!" at the same time. They were all shocked and could not believe that we were together. Pizza Boy took my heavy purse from me and escorted me to a table he'd reserved for us.

Our friends kept asking us all night if we were really together. After a couple drinks it started to irritate me. The aggressive security guard still didn't believe it and pulled out some cash, saying he'd pay to see us kiss because he didn't believe it. I looked at Pizza Boy, who looked like a deer with small eyes, surprised by headlights. I took the cash, leaned over and kissed my man. I kissed him, and he kissed me. People started dropping cash on the table saying "Daaamn, do it again!"

I was starting to love him. I could tell that he felt the same way, but he never said it.

That scared me, so I asked him how he felt about me one day.

Pizza Boy was not good at verbally expressing his feelings. His hugs felt like I was hugging a statue of a boxer with bendable arms, but his actions and everything else screamed, "I love you with everything in me!"

We eventually said that we loved one another.

One night a few months later, I was relaxing at home. I had two jobs at the time and thoroughly enjoyed just being at home and hanging out with my man. Pizza Boy had started working a lot of hours. He liked buying me nice gifts and sending dozens of long-stemmed roses to my job (mainly after disagreements). So, I was at home and getting ready to pick him up from work when I saw Tow Truck Boy riding past my house.

He was yelling while he drove by, "That's messed up, T!" I told one of my girlfriends but never told Pizza Boy because I'd never hear the end of it.

It'd been months since I'd seen Tow Truck Boy. I'd blocked him in my phone and assumed that he'd moved on a while ago. I tried to forget about seeing him that night, but I couldn't shake that feeling of, "OMG, what if he pops up when Pizza Boy is here?!"

I got in my car, and my headlights wouldn't come on. I kept my lights on auto so they should've automatically come on; after all, it was around 11 p.m. But they didn't. My first thought was that Tow Truck Boy did it. I couldn't drive for 30 minutes at night to pick-up Pizza Boy without headlights. I had to tell him what happened.

He got mad, not at me but at the situation, and he got concerned for my safety when he wasn't around.

He was never around. He worked 5-6 evenings a week. He closed the restaurant so he wouldn't get off until after midnight, and sometimes as late as 2 a.m.

I was alone a lot when I wasn't at work. I didn't like it. When we were together, he was completely exhausted. I knew that I should've been understanding, but I wasn't successful all the time.

If I'm being honest, I wasn't ready for a relationship. I shouldn't have been in a relationship with him because I was still in one with my husband. I wasn't ready to take care of someone's heart because mine was still broken. I was antsy when I was alone.

Pizza Boy didn't like my friends. I knew that feeling and refused to let someone isolate me again. I didn't see that he wasn't trying to isolate me. He knew that those "friends" wouldn't tell me when I was wrong. Those "friends" would lie for me and wanted me to be in the streets, clubbing with them. Those "friends" were jealous of our relationship and what he did for me.

He knew these things; I didn't at the time.

Chapter 7

Soul Tie & Exposure

I was out with one of my friends at a seafood restaurant near Baltimore one evening.

I'd filed for divorce, and my nerves were shot. I kept thinking about what my husband would say and do.

This restaurant had karaoke and really good drinks. It was my first time there. It was a good distraction.

I met a guy.

First thought: "Oh no, I have Pizza Boy. No, thank you!" The second thought came from my friend: "Girl, you were with the same man for years! I ain't mad at you, and I ain't sayin' nothing. You know all of those men in Baltimore are hung."

"Really??? Noooo, I shouldn't. I mean, I couldn't, but he is fine!"

I knew that my friend wouldn't tell my boyfriend. She might tell her friends my business, but she'd never tell him.

I figured I could talk to this guy only. He was in Baltimore, which was 30-45 minutes from my grandmother's house. I was not going to see him, and he couldn't come to me, so I'd just talk to him while Pizza Boy was at work.

Pizza Boy had a daughter, a beautiful little girl that he loved dearly. His ex wouldn't let him take their daughter out of her apartment. He was only allowed to sit in her home and spend time with his daughter...well, that's what he said. When our first Thanksgiving came, I asked him what we were going to do: split the day between our families, do Thanksgiving with his family and Christmas with mine? He told me that his father always has a big dinner and he always picks up his ex-girlfriend and his daughter for the dinner. He told me that he was going there, and he said it like I was going to instantly be okay with it.

We'd already had a few arguments about the rules for his visits with his daughter, but this holiday thing was a deal breaker. I'd told Pizza Boy about my history of bad arguments with my husband, but he'd never seen that side of me. It was time.

I let him have it and told him I was done with him, to go be with daughter's mother, because they were still playing house. He could leave me out of it.

We went back and forth about it for over an hour. He left and called me from his father's house, apologizing and agreeing that it was disrespectful because his family agreed with me.

In my mind, it was, "Apology accepted, but the gloves are now off. In other words, I don't trust you. You're doing you, so I'm going to do me."

I started talking to the guy in Baltimore almost daily. Let's call him Bmore.

I'd started gaining weight again since Pizza Boy and I got together. I noticed it and didn't like it, so I purchased an exercise bike and put it in my bedroom at my grandmother's house. I'd wake up early before work, get on the bike and talk to Bmore for 30 minutes or so whenever Pizza Boy wasn't there. Bmore didn't know about Pizza Boy.

A few weeks later, Bmore started pressuring me to come to Baltimore. I told my main girlfriend, and she immediately agreed that I should go hang out with him, and she wanted to go too. She was familiar with the area; I wasn't and I was scared. Bmore said to bring my friend because he didn't want me driving by myself, so I agreed, thinking it was harmless.

Pizza Boy was at work as usual. I told him that my friend and I were going to karaoke, and she and I went to Baltimore. We parked on a residential street. It was quiet but I was leery. My friend reassured me that everything would be okay. She told me to just go sit on the porch and talk with him for a while, to see if I even liked him face-to-face, and then we'd head right back to DC.

He was my height, maybe an inch taller than me, caramel complexioned, slim with strong chiseled facial features, a low and close haircut, piercing eyes and thick lips. He was very laid back, extremely easy to talk to, while remaining aware of his environment like a cheetah ready to pounce.

I was kinda turned on, felt guilty, confused and just like, "What am I doing?" all at the same time.

My cellphone started ringing in my pocket. I looked at it hoping it wasn't Pizza Boy. It was my friend who'd been sitting in the car. She said it'd been two hours and she was ready to go.

Two hours??? I'd been sitting there talking for two hours? I looked at the time, apologized to her repeatedly and told him I had to go. He walked me to my car, met my friend and apologized as well. We hugged and I felt his chiseled body gently hug mine.

I was intrigued.

My friend said "Girl, he's fine and he likes you a lot, but you left me in the car all that time. You didn't check the time? What are you gonna do? I don't mind coming back out here with you sometime if he has a friend." She's so crazy.

I drove her home and called him while I was driving home. He said it was good to see me and wanted us to see one another again soon. Pizza Boy called on the other line. I told Bmore I had to go and went to pick Pizza Boy up from work.

Pizza Boy and I had a regular night. He got into my car, he was tired and his feet were hurting from a long evening at work. He kissed me and told me I looked nice, asked me if I needed him to drive because he knew I'd had a long day as well. I told him I was okay with driving and put my hand on his left thigh as I drove to my grandmother's house. We went inside. He took his shoes off, lay down on my bed and fell asleep immediately with his back turned to me. I got in the bed with my back to him and lay awake, looking out the window.

A few weeks later when Pizza Boy was scheduled to close the restaurant the entire weekend, I decided to spend an evening with Bmore. He was so happy to see me. He tried to keep a cool, nonchalant face, but he kept smiling like a kid in a candy store. We put on a couple movies but ended up talking through both of them. We talked for hours, laughed like two kids that had a crush on one another and eventually locked eyes. We kissed passionately and intensely. He undressed me while he was kissing me, then stood up and quickly undressed himself.

What I'd felt through his clothes was exactly what his reality was. His entire body was chiseled, 8-pack abs, muscular arms, strong neck and chiseled back, smooth and soft skin and overwhelmingly blessed downtown.

We couldn't get enough of one another, over and over, all night and morning. We lay there smiling at one another, talking about who knows what, and then I heard my phone vibrating. It was Pizza Boy; I ignored it.

Reality set in. I'd just cheated on Pizza Boy. That was my first time ever cheating on someone. I'd had relationships when I was in school before I met my husband and still had never cheated on anyone before.

I knew that I should feel bad, but I was still high off of the man that was beside me.

As I drove off, I called my girlfriend.

She didn't even say hello, she just started hollering, "WAS I RIGHT??!!!!"

I said "Giiiiiiiiiirl" and we screamed laughing. I gave her details blow-by-blow as I drove home, ignoring Pizza Boy who was still calling me back to back.

When I got home, I saw that I had 75 missed calls from Pizza Boy. He must not have had more than two hours of sleep that night because the calls were almost nonstop. I told him I was tired when I got home and fell asleep.

This went on for a year. Bmore and I spoke a few days a week and saw one another every couple of weeks or sometimes more frequently. We craved one another in between.

My girlfriend and I had planned to take a cruise together. It was two nights before the cruise, and Pizza Boy and I were together. As usual, he was fresh off of work, tired and I was supposed to understand. I did understand, but I'd also expressed to him my need for attention. That didn't just mean texts and conversations in the car before he passed out. I needed awake time: dates, face-to-face interaction when he was energized, physical activities. He said okay and went to sleep. I said okay and texted Bmore. The next evening and night, I was with Bmore, while Pizza Boy called me back to back from work.

When I returned from the cruise, Pizza Boy acted like he hadn't seen me in years. He apologized and wanted to make it up to me. I said okay but I only half cared. I had been developing feelings for Bmore…intense feelings. He'd told me that he loved me, and I gave him the "deer in headlights" look.

I thought about him all the time. I wanted to be with him all the time. If I thought about him, he'd text within five minutes saying I'd just crossed his mind, and vice versa. If I had a flashback of us being together, he'd call saying he missed me. If I was having sad thoughts, he'd call or text asking if I was okay.

He could feel me and I could feel him.

We had a soul tie.

One day the feelings became too much; I was overwhelmed and needed to come clean. I told Bmore that I was in a relationship and had been for over a year, that I was unhappy and we hardly ever had sex. I'd already told him about my pending divorce when we first met.

He said something like, "Fuck that nigga," and asked when could he come to DC, or when was I coming to Baltimore.

I liked that and hated it. That wasn't who I was. How would I feel if someone did that to me? Well, someone did do it to me.

I decided to block Bmore and stop seeing him. I cried myself to sleep on the nights when I was alone and thought about Bmore after Pizza Boy had fallen asleep. Everything in me was yearning for Bmore, and I was suppressing it.

A couple months later, Pizza Boy took off work so we could go to the lounge where we'd met. We hadn't been there in a year. He was already there when I'd parked outside right after work. My phone rang and I thought it was him. My caller ID said Chrysler Boy.

I answered on the fourth ring. I had to digest the fact that it was him before answering.

I said hello, and his deep smooth voice said, "Hey, how've you been, stranger?" I told him that I was great and that I was heading inside a lounge to meet my boyfriend.

He said, "Oh okay, call me later when he's not around."

He had a lot of nerve!

I walked inside the lounge thinking about what had just happened, Chrysler Boy's sexy voice, how I'd felt about him and missed him, and then I saw Pizza Boy. I hugged and kissed my man and tried to enjoy my night.

An idle mind is the devil's playground.

A few days later, I was at home while Pizza Boy was at work, and Chrysler Boy called again. Pizza Boy was working at a different location now, about an hour away. I would pick him up every night.

Chrysler Boy told me he had moved. A number of things had happened and he had to start over.

I tried to dismiss him, but I couldn't help but wonder, "What if?"

I told my friend, and she asked what I was going to do. She was no help and would always remind me that my boyfriend was always at work.

I was weak and decided to see Chrysler Boy once to talk face-to-face. I went to "his new house" in a very nice neighborhood and he was standing in the doorway waiting for me. He had on a t-shirt, basketball shorts, socks and a house arrest ankle bracelet. I fell out laughing. We sat in front of the fireplace and he caught me up on his last year. I told him I was in a relationship but always alone. I told him that Pizza Boy was always tired and we hardly ever had sex, but that I had to pick him up from work in a few hours.

I could lie right here and try to make myself look like a manipulated victim, but there's freedom in truth.

He wanted me, and I wanted him, but my sober conscience wouldn't let me. He went and got my favorite drink from the kitchen, Patron Silver. I took two shots and we had sex.

We lay together in a blanket, holding one another in front of the fireplace. My iPhone had the flash activated, so my phone would flash when it rang. His living room turned into a strobe light show. Pizza Boy started calling back to back. I checked the time and realized I was supposed to be at his job, picking him up at that moment.

I begged Chrysler Boy to be quiet while I answered the phone. He agreed and immediately started trying to make me moan, laugh, anything while I told Pizza Boy I'd just woke up and was on my way.

I raced to his job and told him I was tired, that I'd had a long day and that I just wanted to go to sleep. He drove us to my grandmother's house. I took a bath and went straight to sleep with a guilty conscience while Pizza Boy held me.

Pizza Boy was off the next day and wanted us to spend some time together. I had a new stereo in my car that he'd purchased and installed. It had a DVD player and a large screen that flipped up and showed the caller ID on it.

We were a few blocks away from Pizza Boy's mother's house. He wanted to pick up some things for our evening. We were going to order takeout and watch movies at my grandmother's house; nothing much, just awake time when neither one of us was tired.

My phone rang, and it was Chrysler Boy. I couldn't grab my phone fast enough so the stereo screen displayed his name while the phone seemed to ring louder than ever through the car stereo. I wanted to pull over and jump out of the car and just walk away, but I was stuck. I was driving, Pizza Boy had seen the caller ID and I hadn't even played it cool.

Pizza Boy said, "Who is that?"

I said, "Huh? Oh, that's a guy I used to talk to before you. We don't talk anymore."

He said, "So why is he still calling you? Does he know about me?"

I said, "I don't know, and no, because we don't talk anymore."

He said, "Call him back! Call him back right now!!!"

I said, "For what? Why?"

He said, "Tameka, do you have something to hide? Call him back!"

I started praying in my head as I slowly called him back, hoping that he'd see I was calling him and believe that nothing was going on.

Jesus, please don't let him pick-up.

Please, Jesus!

Chrysler Boy said, "Hey baby!"

Oh My God! I started sweating. I know I had a dumb look on my face. I could just leave my car right there for a little while. I think Pizza Boy would lock it before he jumped out of it and walked away or tried to come after me.

It felt like the pause between Chrysler Boy saying, "Hey baby," and Pizza Boy responding to him was forever!

Pizza Boy said, "Look man, I don't know who this is, but Tameka has a man now, and I'm asking you man-to-man to stop calling this phone."

I was sitting there with my eyes half closed, peeping at Pizza Boy who was surprisingly calm until Chrysler Boy responded.

Chrysler Boy started laughing at him, and my heart began to sink. Chrysler Boy said, "When you're at work for all those hours, she's with me. Baby, call me later."

I had the "I just stubbed my toe on the side of the bed" look on my face.

Pizza Boy stared at me for a minute while I tried to apologize and explain. He got out of the car and started walking home.

Chapter 8

I Want Better

Pizza Boy and I were on and off for three years.

I got my divorce, and he was there for me every step of the way.

My ex-husband and I both messily brought our significant others to our first divorce hearing. The judge wouldn't allow them in the room with us. My ex-husband was not agreeable at all, so much so that the judge looked at me and said on the record that she felt sorry for me.

We came back for the second hearing, and I'd done what the judge had instructed and more. I had copies of bills, receipts, cancelled checks from items I'd paid off and a proposed payment plan for us to pay off our remaining marital debt. I'd assembled everything into a booklet and had multiple copies of the booklet for everyone. My ex-husband disagreed somewhat this time, and the judge made us go to a room together to discuss and revise the agreement before going upstairs to notarize it and get our divorce finalized.

We were forced to sit in a room alone and talk, for the first time in over almost 2 years.

It was rough. He calmed down as soon as the door closed and we were alone together. He told me that someone in his family had passed away. I said I was so sorry to hear that. He told me about how his niece had grown and asked about my family. I told him that everyone was fine and that I was glad we were able to finally work this out. He apologized for being difficult. We wrote out our agreement slowly, discussed how we would've done some things differently, slowly walked upstairs to get it notarized, came back and got our divorce.

Pizza Boy ended up cheating on me with a young girl that applied to work at his job. He'd forgotten one of his two phones at my grandmother's house and his alarm went off. When I disabled the alarm, the phone unlocked on the text screen, showing his messages to her.

While it's true that I'd done my dirt and I was wrong too, I realized that it was an unhealthy situation for the both of us.

I wanted better. I wanted a fresh start. I was divorced and was over my ex-husband, or so I thought.

I tried to end it with Pizza Boy more than once. He'd always say that he wasn't letting go. I wanted to get married again. I wanted to move into my own apartment, to live alone for the first time or with my man.

Whether he was done with me or not, I was done with him. I found an apartment and asked some of my guy friends to move me.

I moved to a large unrenovated apartment in Greenbelt, Maryland. I was working seven days a week to make ends meet. My grandmother told me she was keeping my dog because I used to work and hangout so much that I was only home during the evenings, and they'd become best friends.

My mother's neighbor was going to take their dog to a shelter because they didn't have time for her anymore. My mother told them about me and that I needed some company, and they paid me to take their shih tzu named Daisy. She ran up to me and jumped onto my lap when she saw me, and she laid her face on my chest. It shocked my mother's neighbor and me, but I knew it was meant to be.

I met a guy who claimed he knew me from a program at my high school. He'd lived in Southeast DC but would come uptown to my school for the program. I was only in school a half day my senior year, so I didn't remember him and didn't fully believe his story. He'd come to my part-time job and bring me lunch, flowers, and sometimes just stand there and keep me company. I was a second shift concierge in an upscale apartment building on the weekends. The residents who were my friends thought he was a nice guy because he was consistent. Let's call him Peppermint.

He was my height, with chocolate skin and an okay smile. He always had a fresh haircut, he smelled nice and he was an architect. He was also separated and had a young daughter. Eh…I wasn't interested.

My birthday came, and he brought a cake and balloons to my full-time job. All of my co-workers said he was nice and had a good career, that I should give him a chance.

Something about him didn't sit right with me, outside of the fact that he was still separated, AKA still married. I couldn't put my finger on it, but everything in me was screaming, "NO. RUN, DON'T DO IT!!!"

I decided to give him a chance. I was afraid of missing my blessing. He seemed to be head over heels in love with me already, so why not?

We dated most Friday nights and started seeing one another frequently. I made him nervous, and it wasn't cute this time like it was with Pizza Boy. I decided to kiss him one night. We'd been dating for weeks, so I figured I'd give it a try just to see. He was a good kisser but immediately started sweating like he was in a marathon. He was nervous and had sweated through his shirt. I still felt like, "Blah," but I was alone and wanted someone there.

I would get stuck at my part-time job on occasion, working 16 hours on Saturday, coming back again on Sunday for my 8-hour shift which ended up being 16 hours sometimes too, then going back to my full-time job on Monday morning.

I was exhausted.

I'd given him my spare key because he'd go feed and walk Daisy when I couldn't make it home. This made me start liking him.

I was in the process of healing from my divorce and ended up going natural, cutting my long, relaxed hair into a short curly fade.

He loved playing in my hair. I smiled while I tried to forgive my ex-husband and figure out how I'd arrived at that point.

I worked so much that I started getting sick once every three months.

Peppermint was persistent and consistent. He was there to take care of me and help me in non-monetary ways whenever I needed him. I started falling for him.

I let him meet all of my friends, my mother and two of my maternal uncles. Everyone was nice to him but let him know that I was recently divorced and to be careful with me. One of my aunts (an uncle's wife) immediately chastised me for dealing with a married man.

Our sex life was okay, not what I was used to, but I wanted to make myself be happy with him.

After months of working seven days a week, and multiple sinus infections, I decided it was time to quit my second job. If I were to quit, I'd only have $2 left every two weeks after paying my bills, buying groceries to make all of my meals and putting enough gas in my car for transportation to/from work only.

I was stressed. I was tired. I was sick. I felt like I was on autopilot. I couldn't take it anymore.

I quit my part-time job and trusted that God would provide. If all else failed, I would buy dog food to make sure my dog could eat, and I'd go eat at my mother's or grandmother's house.

I'd been applying for new full-time jobs for months, and nothing had come through.

Peppermint was right there through it all, at my side. I appreciated him. I cared about him a lot, but I felt like I was forcing myself at times. We had fun in the bedroom but I wasn't completely satisfied.

I decided to unblock Bmore and message him. It had been a year since we'd last spoken and seen one another. I texted him, "Hey."

He responded right away with like 10 text messages:

"What you mean hey"

"Da fuq Tameka"

"Where u been"

"I was just startin to get over you"

"Where are u?"

"I been callin and textin u"

"U musta blocked me"

"Y u decide to reach out now"

"U still wit that nigga?"

"Hello?"

I was crying and reading all of his messages while they were coming through. My heart was still broken from my divorce. The only person I wanted to talk to, that knew about it all and that I felt understood me was Bmore.

I said, "I miss u!"

He said, "U know I'll always miss u and love u. That'll never change, no matter who I'm with."

I started crying and told him. He called me and told me to come to Baltimore right now. He couldn't stand the thought of me being that upset. I told him I was in a relationship and I couldn't. He didn't care, but I did.

I started going back to church and feeling guilty for how I was dealing with Peppermint.

I prayed hard for a new job and about my financial situation, and I even printed and taped the word "PRAY" all around my cubicle as a constant reminder. The word PRAY was taped to my monitor, keyboard, keyboard tray, telephone, mail slots…everywhere I looked I'd see PRAY during my eight-hour work day.

I eventually got a job interview that made me wonder if it was a gift from God.

A colleague called me and asked for my resume. I said sure and emailed it to him while we were on the phone. I asked him what kind of job he was submitting it for and he dismissed my question. Umm…okay.

That afternoon a young lady called me to schedule the interview. We found a day and time, and I asked her what job I'd be interviewing for. She said, "Do you want it or not?" I said yes but started second-guessing the idea of going to the interview. She had a bad attitude, and I was going in blind. The only thing I could do to prepare for the unknown was to pray.

I didn't get the job as the Assistant Property Manager that I interviewed for because the Vice President told me I was overqualified. However, I ended up mentoring the manager that was part of the interview and getting referred for the Vice President's old position in Richmond, Virginia.

Less than four weeks after I'd quit my second job, I received an offer for a senior-level position that nearly doubled my salary.

I'd stepped out on faith by quitting my second job, knowing that my financial success was only barely possible. God then blessed me beyond what I could've asked for, imagined or thought.

As soon as I received the offer in writing, I knew that it was time to break it off with Peppermint.

We had dinner, and I told him that I can't do a long-distance relationship. I said I thought that we should just be friends. We talked about it for a while, and he reluctantly agreed.

I went home and cried myself to sleep. I was relocating in one week and didn't have a lot of time to bask in my confused sadness, but I did have time to tell Bmore. I called him and shared my good news. He was happy that I was happy but sad that I was going so far.

Two nights before my move, I went out with some friends to celebrate. Two drinks later I excused myself to go to the bathroom. What was happening?!? New job, new city, all alone and in two days. Everything was happening so fast, which I was grateful for, but I wanted to see the one person that I still loved before I left — Bmore. I texted him from the club saying I wanted to see him. He said he was waiting for me.

First stop: I swung by Peppermint's apartment and got my spare key.

Second stop: Baltimore.

Chapter 9

A Fresh Start, I Think…

There I was, sitting in my brand-new apartment. The community was literally still being built. I lived in one of the first four buildings that'd been completed. The area was beautiful and so quiet the insects seemed loud at night. The sky was bright and clear; the stars seemed to stand out. I was in awe of God's creation and had no one to enjoy it with.

I'd walk Daisy, come back inside and unpack. I had a full week before I started my new job. Outside of talking to friends and family when they weren't working, I was forced to be with myself and Jesus.

I didn't talk to any of the guys except for Bmore.

I was so lonely, but I talked to God frequently, thanking Him for answering my prayer for a new job. I wanted to make sure God knew that I wasn't being ungrateful. Isolation just wasn't part of my plan.

After a few days of unpacking, sightseeing and shopping, I settled into my new home. It was beautiful, and I was proud of myself. I decided to focus on and bask in this feeling.

I started my new job. My coworkers were so laid back and chill. I had a large cubicle and a number of technological devices, and I found out that I'd be traveling a lot. Talk about excited!

I've always been an emotional eater. Since I didn't have anyone to share my happiness with face-to-face, I ate my feelings. Fifteen pounds later, irritation, extreme loneliness and disappointment set in.

I resisted the urge to reach out to Peppermint, although everything in me was screaming, "CALL HIM!"

The loneliness got so bad that I started asking my friends to visit me because I couldn't take it anymore. My best girlfriend came down to visit from New York. I was beyond grateful! We had so much fun for days, acting like high school kids and laughing most of the night. I cried like a baby when she left. She told me to start exploring my new city and to not be afraid of going out by myself.

She was right.

Richmond was beautiful! It felt like people stared at me when I was out in public, but I still loved my new city. It'd been weeks and I hadn't made any friends, although I'd attended functions and went out frequently.

I was so lonely I couldn't take it anymore. All I could do was work, pray and cry. Then one day Peppermint called me. He asked how I was doing, about my new place and new job. I broke down. We talked all night and every day for the next few days.

Peppermint came down to visit that weekend. He hugged me tight and smelled so good. I latched onto him and didn't want to let go. Outside of college, this was my first time really being away from loved ones. It was so hard for me. I felt like no one understood, and I just needed someone there.

Peppermint sensed my feelings and missed me too, ultimately deciding to come visit me a few days a week. He still worked in DC and lived in Maryland. His job was about two hours from where I lived, yet he would still come to Richmond a few days a week, even commuting to/from work a couple days a week.

His visits weren't enough for him. He wanted to move to Richmond.

Part of me knew it was a bad idea. I felt like God had helped me get away from him, by moving me to Richmond, and I was inviting him back into my life again. I ignored my gut instinct, and we moved into a larger apartment in the same community together. He would drive my car two hours each way every day and maintain his same job. His daughter would come and stay with us every other weekend and had her own bedroom.

It was blissful for a couple months, until he got tired of the drive. He kept telling me that he was tired and that I didn't understand how the commute was wearing on his body. He started catching colds, which was uncommon for him. He was still going through his divorce and began having frequent court appearances and required mediation sessions.

Our relationship started to change. I could tell that his heart was starting to lean back toward his wife. She started leaving him long emotional voicemails and send video messages, saying what his absence was doing not only to her, but also to their daughter. He looked to me for comfort. I would try to physically console him, but I felt horrible.

He had been telling me that he and I should start our family as soon as possible, but at this point my heart ached for his daughter, his one and only child. If he could leave his wife and his only child to be with me, he had the potential to turn around and do the same thing to me and possibly our future children one day.

For months, I had been praying for God to bless our mess of a relationship but now my prayer was different. I told God that I felt bad for what I'd gotten myself into and that I felt stuck. I didn't see a way out, and I knew that he wasn't the right one for me.

A few months later his divorce was finalized. The entire process of divorce, child support, mediation, visitation and his wife harassing him and playing on my phone was draining.

A few weeks later, my father got sick and passed away. Peppermint was physically present, but his hugs weren't hugs. He would wrap his arms around me, but he was stone cold. There were no feelings there anymore on his end when I needed him the most. He told me I should call my girlfriends to come down and be with me, and he decided to go clubbing one night. He came home from DC smelling like a bottle of liquor, and I wasn't sure how he made the drive. Over the next couple days, he became extremely secretive, taking his phone with him every time he moved and suspiciously dropping it when I entered the room.

One night, he didn't come home at all and didn't answer his phone when I called.

A day later, he came home and said he was going to move closer to DC — alone. In other words, he was breaking up with me...ten days after my father had passed away.

I hadn't eaten in days. I had horrible acid reflux. I could barely sleep. All of this was the result of me grieving my father.

When I heard this news from Peppermint, I said okay and pulled my tablet out of the top drawer of the dresser. When he had failed to come home the night before, I made out a plan for us to separate and pay off the little bit of living expenses we had together because I was done with him. I responded to him saying that was a good idea, that I had already mapped out a plan to split things up financially and that he needed to move out like yesterday.

He started looking crazy. He and I had never really argued, so he had never seen my crazy side. My mother had warned him more than once in a joking way, which I think contributed to him getting the nerve to express himself a bit, while I wasn't at 100%. He started to escalate a little with me from across the room, so I sat up and said, "You don't want it. Trust me, you don't want it." That was me letting him know that it was time for him to simmer his attitude down. Although I was grieving, I was beyond willing to use all of the energy I had left to let his ass have it!

How dare he leave me when I needed him the most! While it's true that he was there to comfort me when I first moved, I'd been his girlfriend, lawyer, therapist and financial advisor for months through his divorce process.

My indifferent feelings toward him, him not coming home some nights, coming home extremely late other nights, and sleeping in a different bedroom were huge distractions from grieving. All of my family and friends were pissed. I decided to call Bmore and confide in my good friend…we'd established that we were, umm, "best friends" or something and hadn't spoken since Peppermint moved to Richmond. I'd blocked Bmore because Peppermint had been telling me, my family and friends how much he loved me and couldn't wait to marry me.

I Facetimed Bmore, and he picked up almost immediately. He started fussing at me as soon as I told him what had happened. Bmore felt horrible about what I was going through and told me to come to Baltimore to see him. When Peppermint walked into the bedroom, I looked at him and continued my conversation. Peppermint and I didn't talk anymore, unless absolutely necessary. He initiated the silent treatment, and I just went along with it. I knew that it further confirmed that God was helping me out, once again.

That night I prayed for God to show me my purpose. I knew that there was something that God had put inside of me, a gift, a calling, purpose…something, but I didn't know what it was. I woke up that morning and God said, "Hey Giirl!" I said, "God, I know, but I can't do it right now." I was broken! My father had just passed, my boyfriend who I thought would be my husband was leaving, and I was angry at myself for inviting him back into my life. I couldn't start a business to help anyone right now because I needed to help myself.

I started going to the gym every night. I'd do 20-60 minutes of cardio, come home get in the shower and go to work like everything was okay, because it was going to be.

I went to New York to be with my best girlfriend for Valentine's Day. She and I were both single, so I figured it'd be a good idea to hang with her for a few days. I took Daisy to my mother's house in DC. I forgot to mention that Daisy had started ignoring Peppermint too. I'd started to wonder if he was mean to her when I wasn't at home, so I tried to make sure those potential alone moments were rare if they happened at all.

When I returned from New York, Peppermint had disassembled all of the furniture he'd purchased, which included all of the master bedroom furniture and dining room furniture. I'd sold part of my bedroom furniture when we moved in together, but I still had a bed and chest of drawers that were in his daughter's room, and all of the living room furniture and TV were mine.

A week later, he came in early one Saturday morning with his brother and they moved his things. I'd started losing weight and felt so proud of myself. I was looking forward to peace of mind. When they got down to the last few things of his, I got up and held the door for them. He and I didn't speak for the entire move until his last trip inside the apartment. I told him that he needed to take his keys to the leasing office before he left and sign the form to have his name taken off the lease. He said okay and I closed the door in his face, while he was picking up his last box off the ground in front of the door.

I started thanking God immediately and asking for His forgiveness, and then I called the leasing office to confirm that they'd received the keys and the signed form. They had.

I blessed my apartment and promised God and myself that I'd do better going forward.

Let the work begin.

Chapter 10

Who Am I?

There I was, alone again.

This time felt different.

I was alone, but I wasn't lonely.

It felt like my mother and friends were grieving the loss of my relationship for me, but I was fine. They were constantly checking on me, saying how angry they were. I had to tell them to get over it because I had.

I'd started hanging out more, doing productive things like attending self-help seminars and workshops, going to exercise classes at an all-women's gym where I made new friends, and started to really enjoy my own company.

I met a profound young lady at a conference that my friend hosted, and she pulled me to the side afterward to tell me that she saw herself in me. She gave me a free copy of her book and told me to read the chapter on codependency.

Reading was always a passion of mine, but reading about codependency was like holding a mirror up to my last year. That's why I'd allowed Peppermint back into my life. I needed someone to fill me up, to depend on, to be my crutch, and in the process, I was sucking the life out of him while he was sucking the life out of me. I had been a codependent empath, and he was a narcissist.

That was a hard pill to swallow. I didn't like seeing myself in that light. I was happy to start becoming more self-aware, but at the same time, it made me angry with myself. Why couldn't I see? Why didn't I know? What else did I have going on that I wasn't aware of?

I started to journal. I took my time and patiently and candidly answered these questions:

Who am I, not what are my roles or what hats do I wear, but who am I?

Are any of these things genetic, generational curses/cycles/habits?

What do I need to unlearn?

In what areas do I need to grieve, heal and forgive?

In what areas do I need to re-parent myself?

What do I like? What makes me happy?

What does self-care look like for me?

What are my current boundaries and what adjustments are needed?

What areas can I work on now, on my own, with God's help of course?

In what areas do I need to get help?

My mother brought me new furniture for my master bedroom and a chaise lounge for my meditation room, formerly Peppermint's daughter's room. My neighbor gave me her dining room table and chairs because she was refurnishing her place, which made my apartment fully furnished — for free! Won't He Do It!

The second book on my list: *Year of Yes* by Shonda Rhimes. That was a game changer for me!

It felt like Shonda Rhimes was my twin sister. I could relate to almost everything from her being a

Capricorn (me too, giirl) to her fears and her thought process. I highlighted so much of that book and still have flags sticking out, going around the entire perimeter of the book. If Shonda (she's my friend in my head) could say "yes" to everything for a year, so could I.

My first yes: Yes, to who I really am.

I am the daughter of a young mother. I was validated by a caring family so much that I never had to figure out who I was, until now. I am a perfectionist scaredy-cat that has anxiety and stutters when I get nervous, afraid or anxious. I am a materialist, enjoying luxury items and experiences that seemingly provide a certain level of status. I sought fulfillment from men, first through my marriage and then through the men afterward to put a bandage on the emptiness and void that none of them would ever be qualified to fill – a void that only God and I could fill. I am an emotional eater who mindlessly eats during times of boredom, stress, loneliness and even happiness. I am an empathic person that can feel the emotions of others, and at times I try to fix the person whenever and however I can. I am a people pleaser. I had been willing to sacrifice myself for love, completely overlooking my wants, needs and loved ones to focus on the person that I was in a relationship with. I had low self-esteem because of my weight, because I didn't love myself or even know myself. I didn't respect myself, so how could I expect someone else to?

All of these were painful epiphanies.

I didn't like who I had unknowingly become and I had to change it — immediately.

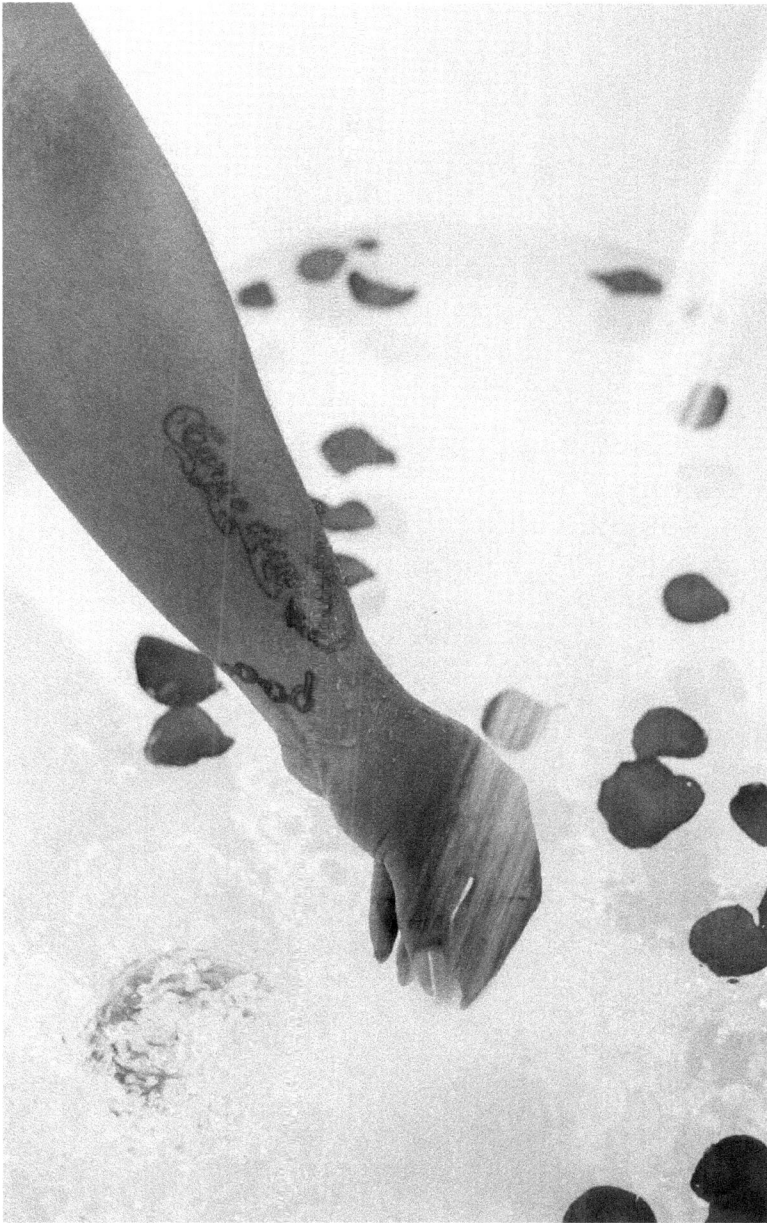

Chapter 11

Jezebel Spirit

I've always been an intense person. When I love someone or have my mind set on a task, I focus and work hard at it. I fight for what I want and who I love.

It was time to fight for myself.

As I began to spend more time alone, I starting becoming more self-aware and even more aware of how people respond to me.

A lot of women didn't like me and a lot of men, including married men, gravitated toward me. I used to think the male portion was cute during my separation and before Peppermint, but now something didn't seem right.

I knew that I didn't want to deal with any man that was married, separated or even divorced for less than a year; yet, it seemed like married men and men in ministry seemed to be attracted to me the most. Attending church was a hassle because married men would stare at me, causing their wives to hate me and collectively isolate me. When I went out, married men would look in my eyes and smile, even stare at me in front of their wives. I'd get preferential treatment, catered to, and I received inappropriate sexual advances. All of it made me just want to hide.

It even happened on a group vacation once. I was in Jamaica, sitting at the bar with one of my girlfriends. A few of the couples in our group came into the bar. I noticed that one of the husbands was staring at me from across the room. I tried to ignore it and tell myself that I was imagining it because his wife was standing right beside him. A few minutes later he stood up, looking straight in my face and said out loud for everyone in the entire bar to hear: "Man, if I wasn't a married man, I'd take you to my room right now and wear you out!!!" His wife grabbed him and immediately dragged him out of the bar, while he kept saying "What? What?" The wife, her husband and all of their closest friends avoided me for the remainder of the trip. All I was doing was sitting at the bar, laughing and talking with my girlfriend.

I began to feel extremely uncomfortable every time I left my apartment, and i didn't like it. I started wearing loose, baggy clothes to try and hide my curves, and I stopped wearing makeup. I tried to stop making eye contact with men. I'd look down when married men were around and only made eye contact when absolutely necessary. I just wanted to be invisible.

Even with my adjustments, the inappropriate attention didn't stop. On top of it, I was still young and my hormones were racing, especially when it was time for my cycle to come.

Although it already felt like I was isolated, I began to isolate myself even more.

One day one of my friends posted on Facebook that someone needed to get rid of her Jezebel spirit. I don't know if she was talking about me but a light bulb came on.

How sneaky and dangerous…I'd been dealing with a Jezebel spirit for Lord knows how long, and I didn't even know it.

The Jezebel spirit likes leaders, people that are charismatic, people that are intelligent and attractive. It will attach itself to you, you won't even know and it will try to use you to cause conflict, separation and disruption in godly relationships and environments.

Not only had it been using me, but it was diminishing me in the process — but not anymore. Now that I knew what it was, it was time to fight!

I got on my knees.

Father God, I humbly approach Your throne of grace

First thanking You for being God and God all by Yourself.

There is no other like You!

You are Alpha and Omega, the beginning and the end.

You are the creator of it all and I kneel in awe of You.

Lord God, I believe there's been a Jezebel spirit attacking me and I need Your help.

You said in Your word that there's power in the name of Jesus,

In Philippians 2:10 that at the name of Jesus, every knee shall bow

Of those in heaven, of those on earth and those under the earth.

So I'm praying right now in Jesus' mighty name that You release me from the Jezebel spirit. I rebuke it right now in the name of Jesus. I rebuke its stronghold on my life and take back my peace, my innocence, and my life in the name of Jesus. Jezebel, you have NO PLACE HERE!!

Father God I pray that You protect me and increase my discernment and wisdom from this day forward.

I thank You for freeing me and giving me Your peace.

I pray all these things in Jesus' mighty name, amen.

"Therefore, if the Son makes you free, you are free indeed." – John 8:36

Chapter 12

I Can't Do This on My Own

Months had gone by. I'd read multiple books. I was enjoying life for the first time in years.

During the months after I'd prayed to be released from the Jezebel spirit, the married men immediately left me alone. I felt free in that aspect and began to dress like myself again.

I'd met a guy...a single guy...and he and I began to spend time with one another. I knew he wasn't the one but I enjoyed having non-married man company, and let's be honest, I wanted to get physical. So, I did.

I enjoyed it during the physical moments and felt guilty immediately after.

I knew he wasn't the person I'd spend my life with, that he wasn't the man that God had for me. However, he satisfied a need. We weren't in a relationship, and we didn't do a lot of relationship-type of things. We just spent time together and got physical.

I felt a little emotionally numb, yet I wasn't so numb that I couldn't acknowledge that the bit of numbness was a problem.

As I mentioned, I'm a perfectionist. I'd been trying to celebrate my progress but I couldn't because something didn't feel right.

I kinda knew what the something was, but I couldn't bring myself to articulate it.

I'd started complaining a lot. Whenever someone would ask me how I was doing, I'd tell them. I mean, they asked, right? I'd say I was stressed or tell them what was getting on my nerves in detail if they were close to me. It got so bad it felt like people were avoiding me because all I did was complain.

I remember sitting in my hotel room. I was out of town attending a work conference, and I was tired and fed up. I was tired of being a friend with benefits. I was tired of dealing with guys just for the sake of having somebody there. I was tired of being taken for granted and feeling misunderstood. I was tired of complaining and I'm pretty sure everyone around me was tired of hearing it too. I was fed up!

Misunderstood...how could I say that I felt misunderstood when I didn't even understand myself at that moment?

Did anyone really see me? Did any of these guys care about me? Did I even care about myself?

I felt needy, and I didn't like it.

I loved myself, right? I valued myself and knew my worth, right? I think so, I mean...I guess. I'd never really thought about it before. In my mind self-love was supposed to be automatic.

That night and through tears, I told God that I needed His help. I'd done all that I could do on my own; although I'd made progress, I still felt incomplete and like something was wrong.

God said, "Go to therapy." I said, "Black people don't go to therapy." God said again, "Go to therapy."

I googled therapists in my area, read some profiles and found someone that specialized in stress management and emotional eating. Perfect, that's exactly what I felt were the core of my issues.

I emailed the therapist and told her as much of my business as I could fit into three paragraphs. I figured three was a good number. I didn't want to tell her so much that she'd think I was a hot mess and wouldn't take me on as a new client.

The next day she replied saying that my needs are her specialty; however, she was fully booked for the year but expects to have some availability at the beginning of the next year. That was months away!

I cried and said, "God, you told me to go to therapy!!! I found a therapist who seemed perfect and she's not available!"

God said, "Wait for her." So, I did.

During the months of waiting, I continued to read books: *GirlBoss* by Sophia Amoruso, and *You Do You: How to Be Who You Are and Use What You've Got to Get What You Want* by Sarah Knight, and *Big Magic: Creative Living Beyond Fear* by Elizabeth Gilbert, to name a few.

In the first week of January 2018, I emailed the therapist again. At this point, I was beyond emotionally exhausted. She emailed me right back saying that ironically, she had one opening on Fridays at lunchtime. That was perfect! I could go on my lunch breaks and no one would know.

I went to therapy once every two weeks.

I bared my soul. I cried. I had epiphanies. I cried some more. I wept and I did the work because I was determined to fight for my future.

Therapy was my dump as well as my construction ground. I dug up the roots from my childhood: the validation, fear of judgment and some realizing that because of it all, I didn't love myself.

How could I expect someone to love me when I didn't love myself?

We show the world how to love us based on the way we love ourselves.

Sure, I dressed well, but I was putting clothes on top of an empty and hurt mess.

Once again, I didn't like what I was realizing about myself. This time, I had someone to hold my hand and coach me through the process. I would not beat myself up this time. Instead, I would be gentle with myself. I would be kind to myself. I would comfort myself and finally forgive myself.

I forgave myself for unknowingly making decisions that would negatively affect me.

I forgave myself for staying in my marriage longer than I probably should have stayed.

I forgave myself for the other guys and for allowing Peppermint in my life, even though I knew he wasn't the one for me.

I forgave myself for making decisions out of loneliness.

I did the best that I could do with the knowledge and life experience I had at that time.

I refused to beat myself up, instead choosing to love myself through it all.

I started writing in a gratitude journal. Every morning I would find one thing to be grateful for and I'd write it down. I started going to bed earlier because my body needed good rest. I made doctor appointments to take care of my health concerns and for routine check-ups. I started drinking more water and feeding myself better foods. I became kinder, peaceful and even more empathetic toward others. I'm already a softy, but this was on another level.

I was finally loving me, which enabled me to better love others.

Chapter 13

Generational Curses & Habits

A lot of who we are isn't really us. A lot of what we do isn't really us. A lot of how and why isn't really us.

It's genetic and generational.

If you look in the mirror, who do you look like?

A lot of our habits and mannerisms come from those that raised us. We begin to sound like our parents eventually and even respond in the same ways, even when those responses aren't the best. They're just our default.

I decided to take some time to think about my family habits, hindrances and potential generational curses. I know that both my mother and father have bad tempers, along with some of my uncles on my mother's side. I was okay in this category until my ex-husband happened. Pride is an issue for both of my parents and uncles on my mother's side. I'm not so bad in this category, but while we're taming monsters I might as well get a hold of this little one too. Both of my parents like nice things...yeah, yeah...I'm materialistic. Anxiety and fluctuating weight are both issues on my mother's side. And last but not least, sexual addiction is a problem on my mother's side.

So we've got: temper, pride, materialism, anxiety, weight and sex. Help, Jesus!

The Bible says that we have free will, so everything in life is a choice. Regardless of what you're predisposed to do, you can choose to live a better/different life.

My temper surfaced when I was forced to defend myself. Now that I'm no longer in that situation, I don't need to keep my anger switch on the Ready position. There's no need to argue unnecessarily. I can choose to pick my battles. If I'm always fussing/complaining/barking about something, people will begin to associate negativity with my name. They'll start expecting it and treating me like an unhappy, angry person. I can choose peace, locking away my temper for survival and protection instances only. A soft answer turns away wrath.

Pride is a tricky one. Some, including myself, interpret this as independence. I know that I can handle a lot, but even when I need help, I'll still try to get it done or make a way on my own because I don't want to ask for help. I feel like I'm letting myself down and showing weakness f I can't handle everything and have an answer for everything. You see, all of us need someone. We weren't created to do life alone, and I'm not just talking about marriage. No one is good at everything. You might thrive in one category or in a few, but there may be someone that's a genius in an area where you're lacking. Ask for their help. Get their advice. Hire them. Befriend them. Life is not a solo mission, and this is not a one-woman show. You'll be happy that you denied your pride later, and I'm sure you'll create new relationships and strengthen existing ones by showing your humanity.

Surprisingly, materialism was easy for me. I made big drastic changes, and I made them immediately. I did some research and decided to adopt a minimalist approach to life. Drastic, I know. I sold a lot of items on Craigslist and Facebook Marketplace. I also sold a couple of items to my neighbors' daughter and donated a number of things to Purple Heart. I can be extreme when I'm ready to change or improve. Why waste time? I reviewed my wardrobe and made a list of basic items that I needed, that could be worn a number of ways and could cross seasons. I did a little bit of shopping to build my capsule wardrobe and stopped spending money on the unnecessary. I still dressed nice and had accumulated some classic pieces and accessories over time. And since I loved myself now, I no longer had to dress a certain way to mask or attempt to prove anything.

Anxiety, now this was a hard one. I had to create and maintain a morning routine. I don't like to rush in the mornings. Starting my day in a hurried way makes me anxious. My routine includes waking up in peace, stretching, praying, meditating, my gratitude journal, exercise and a relaxing shower with music and a candle. Although that might sound like a lot, it takes less than 2 hours. If you ask me or anyone that has dealt with anxiety in any way, it's worth it. Even if you're not anxious, if you're stressing or feeling overwhelmed, creating a morning routine is a game changer. It will calm your seas and allow you to flow.

Weight loss has been an issue for most of my life. I know I'm an emotional eater, craving sweets when I crave love, salt when I'm irritated, and so on. On top of it all, I'm a feeler. In other words, my heart has just as much input as my mind and will override the system at times. If I don't feel like eating right or working out, there's a chance that it might not happen. Notice that this is present tense because this still takes conscious effort. To help alleviate some of the stress in this category, I've hired a personal trainer and I've paid for a health coach to keep me accountable with my eating. Forget pride, I'm trying to be "summer time fine," and I want to have some of my back out when I get married again one day.

And finally, sex. Help, Jesus...I'm so serious. Rough day at work, sex. Life feeling a little stressful, sex. Had a couple of cocktails, sex. Feeling sexy in these boy shorts, sex. Had a memory of...sex, but what does that accomplish? It's just instant gratification, a sin because I'm not married and a wet bandage on top of the real issues. There are other ways to cope, healthy ways. First step, I had to eliminate the temptation. Ol' boy that I was dealing with had to go, so I cut him off. I had to pray about that, I even cried a little bit grieving the loss of, umm, that. I had to unfollow some folks on social media, mainly celebrities that I would lust after. I had to filter my music because certain types of songs would send my hormones into overdrive. If it weren't already obvious, I'd decided to become celibate, so no sex and no masturbation. If this is an issue that you have as well, giirl, don't fall out on me. Celibacy is not only possible, it's a form of self-respect and self-love. Most of these guys aren't deserving of that level of access to us anyway. We barely know these guys, we don't know their history and issues and end up laying with them, creating soul ties and attaching all of their known and unknown messes to us. Then we wonder why we're getting new cravings, new habits and can't stop thinking about these guys. We're creating unhealthy soul ties, which aren't easy to break. Been there, done that and no thanks. Nowadays, I know the power of sex. I know what I bring to the table in that category, and I'm confidently protecting and preserving that for the husband that God has for me. When strong cravings and temptation come, if you aren't able to resist on your own, then pray and get yourself an accountability partner. Reduce alcohol consumption.

Is it easy? Not every day is easy, but most days it is. Either way, it's worth it.

All of this takes conscious effort. When instances arise and I'm tempted, I have to literally take a breath. My default traits wanted to respond for a while, but as I continued to deny the urge to do what came naturally, I reprogrammed myself and created new defaults.

I could no longer justify my mess anyway. I knew better. It was time to be better.

Chapter 14

All In!!!

God, I'm in complete awe of You!

As I look in the mirror, I see a woman that I never knew I could be. I see a strong woman, a courageous woman, a woman that embraces her sensitivity and finally sees it as the strength that it actually is.

I see a woman that's not afraid to be vulnerable. I see a woman that's whole. I see a woman that's unapologetic about her peace and boundaries. I see a woman that's not afraid to love. I see a woman that took the risks, while full of fear, to do the work on herself. I see a woman swimming in overflow and I see a woman that yearns to give others what you've given her.

A few months after I'd been going to therapy, I woke up and heard God say "Hey Giirl."

I sat up, opened the Notes in my phone and immediately searched for Hey Giirl. I knew that I'd heard it before, maybe more than once. The search pulled up a couple of notes, all in the same month and once every two years I'd typed: "I woke up and heard God say Hey Giirl." That was a sign.

God, I hear you, and this time — I'm ready!

I grabbed a pen and a notebook and began to write.

What is Hey Giirl? Hey Giirl is an instant friend, advice guru and confidant service. It's a safe place for women to vent and receive empathetic input that they can apply to their situations.

How will Hey Giirl operate? I will create a website where women can schedule a time to chat. I'll call them saying "Hey Giirl" and be the ear, shoulder, coach or big sister that they need. I will write a book one day soon, sharing my testimony and pouring from the overflow of love and light that God has given me.

How will Hey Giirl impact the world? I envision a world where no woman feels alone. A world where women see and know themselves, where women love with wisdom and understanding, thriving as the powerful creations that we are. Hey Giirl will be the catalyst in the self-actualization, "women as a village" movement.

I feel so empowered, reading the words that I just wrote.

The Bible says in Habakkuk 2:2 to "write the vision and make it plain on tablets, that he may run who reads it. For the vision is yet for an appointed time; But at the end it will speak, and it will not lie. Though it tarries, wait for it; Because it will surely come, It will not tarry."

This is my appointed time.

www.HeyGiirl.com

Epilogue

Sometimes when you think you've finished doing what God told you to do, He says "Keep going, you're not done yet." God's ideas; His flow.

I thought I was finished writing this book at Chapter 9 or 10. God said, "No, now that you've told them your shenanigans, it's time to give your testimony. Tell them how I brought you out. Tell them how I delivered you, how I opened your eyes. Tell them how I changed you. Tell them how I'm using you."

God has allowed me to see how my vulnerability is helping women to exit bad situations, to become who they really are, to give themselves permission to put themselves first.

I'd love to end my book by saying that all that I've prayed for has come, that I'm happily married with three beautiful children and I'm solely employed by God and myself. I'd love to…but it hasn't happened just yet. HOWEVER, God gave me a couple of things to do first and told me a secret.

Has God given you something to do?

Maybe you thought it seemed too big or impossible. Maybe you're like me and have been saying "Who me???" for years.

YOUR OBEDIENCE is the master key to your destiny.

Stop blaming God for your delays and do what He told you to do. Stop wondering if that was really God that said it. Yeah giirl, it was!!! You didn't hear Him wrong and no, you're not losing your mind. It was God. NOW DO IT!!!

Build it, do it and watch God bless it!!!

If you need someone to come alongside you, take her earrings off, put on her Vaseline and fight with you, Reach Out To Me.

You are NOT alone. You do NOT have to take this journey alone, and no, you're NOT the only person that's ever been in that situation. Don't be ashamed.

You've Got This!!!

Blessings, love and light.

Tameka

Founder & Owner of Hey Giirl, LLC

www.HeyGiirl.com

Facebook: HeyGiirlfriend

Instagram: @HeyGiirlfriend

#Validated